FROM THE AUTHOR OF
*PREMIUM FINANCED LIFE INSURANCE
THE KEY TO EFFECTIVE ESTATE TAX PLANNING*

IUL

For Aspiring Know-It-Alls

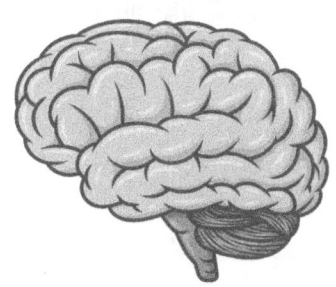

DARREN SUGIYAMA

DARREN SUGIYAMA

IUL For Aspiring Know-It-Alls
Darren Sugiyama
Copyright © 2024
ISBN: 978-1-304-078551

Table Of Contents

Chapter 1: Dummies... pg. 5

Chapter 2: Wealthy People..................................... pg. 9

Chapter 3: Policy Charges..................................... pg. 19

Chapter 4: Floors & Caps...................................... pg. 25

Chapter 5: Policy Drawdowns................................... pg. 33

Chapter 6: Multiplier Bonuses................................. pg. 39

Chapter 7: Backtesting.. pg. 45

Chapter 8: Volatility Controlled Indices...................... pg. 57

Chapter 9: My Own IUL... pg. 65

Chapter 10: History Of The Author............................. pg. 69

Disclaimer:

The author of this book is not a CPA or tax attorney. Nothing in this book shall be misconstrued as tax advice or legal advice. For any tax-related or legal-related questions or concerns, it is highly recommended that you consult your CPA, tax professional, or tax attorney regarding these specific topics.

Chapter 1
Dummies

Most life insurance agents are *dummies*. In today's hyper-sensitive environment, I'm sure this statement will offend a lot of people... but that doesn't mean it isn't true.

It is absolutely true.

Any *dummy* can take an online course, pass a very simple exam, and bingo... they're a licensed insurance agent.

In the state of California where I live, the passing score on this licensing exam is only 60%. So if a *dummy* gets a *D-* grade on their exam, they become licensed – by the state of California – to give financial advice when it comes to life insurance.

Talk about a low barrier to entry.

In addition, the life insurance industry does a terrible job of educating insurance agents how life insurance products *actually* work in real world scenarios – good, bad, and ugly.

I have even heard some life insurance training programs encourage agents to K.I.S.S. (an acronym for *Keep It Simple Stupid*). Though I understand that many clients that buy life insurance are neither mathematical geniuses nor financial gurus, I believe that clients deserve the right to fully understand what they are buying. Consumer protection should be rooted in client education, and if licensed professionals are supposed to be giving clients financial advice as it pertains to life insurance, shouldn't they be experts in the products they are recommending?

Of course they should, but they are not.

Most of them are *product dummies*.

To make matters even worse, there is a high level of righteous indignation that many life insurance agents embody. Some are hardcore *IUL Enthusiasts* despite their veneer understanding of how the *IUL* product chassis is *actually* constructed. On the other side of the aisle are the *IUL Haters* that say *IULs* are too risky. These *Anti-IUL Zealots* are equally as ignorant.

The same could be said about *Whole Life Enthusiasts* and *Haters*, *Term Insurance Enthusiasts* and *Haters*, and *Variable Universal Life Enthusiasts* and *Haters*.

The truth of the matter is that each one of these life insurance product categories is suitable for a very specific client demographic. But the reality is, most clients do not own the appropriate life insurance product, largely because it was sold to them by a life insurance agent that didn't truly understand the product they sold.

Imagine if there was a world where doctors only had to take a 52-hour online course and score a *D-* on their licensing exam in order to get a medical license. Now imagine this *so-called doctor* prescribing drugs to their patients without truly understanding the potential benefits AND risks of certain pharmaceuticals. That would be crazy.

But this is the reality that exists in the world of life insurance right now – a bunch of *dummies* selling insurance products they don't understand to unsuspecting clients – clients who are ALSO *dummies* when it comes to life insurance planning.

This harsh reality is the reason why I wrote this book.

IUL For Aspiring Know-It-Alls is the twelfth book I have authored in my career, with my works being distributed in fourteen different countries in addition to the United States.

One of my books – **Premium Financed Life Insurance - The Key To Effective Estate Tax Planning** – reviews a very sophisticated estate tax planning strategy called *Premium Financing*. This is a life insurance strategy often times used by clients whose net worth is over $25 million in which they borrow seven-figure premiums from a bank, similar to buying real estate using a mortgage loan. In that book, I extensively review a life insurance product called *Indexed Universal Life (IUL)*, and though the targeted audience for that book is the uber-wealthy, my articulation of how *IULs* actually work could certainly be applied to smaller non-financed policies, hence the impetus to release this book – *IUL For Aspiring Know-It-Alls*.

Many of the chapters in this book are taken right out of my **Premium Financed Life Insurance** book. I have removed the chapters and content that only talk about the financing of premiums, so this book you are reading now – *IUL For Aspiring Know-It-Alls* – focuses on a non-financed version of the same *IUL* product.

Perhaps you are wondering what gives me the authority to talk so bluntly (and somewhat harshly) about these issues. I realize that calling someone a *dummy* can certainly come off as being arrogant and condescending. To be clear, my intention is not to bash other *insurance professionals* nor to bash the intellect and financial sophistication of *insurance clients*, rather my true intention is to be a beacon of truth in this industry and teach both advisors and clients how *IULs* actually work in real world scenarios.

I recently heard the head of a large life insurance organization say, *"That Sugiyama guy... he won't even sugarcoat a cookie."* This cracked me up, however it is absolutely true. In today's world that promotes over-political correctness, I have built a reputation in this industry as being a disruptor, a truth teller, and a man of honor that is not afraid to transparently show people the indisputable math – the actual *truth* – when it comes to certain life insurance product designs.

If you would like to learn more about my professional background and credentials, the final chapter of this book will explain my journey in this industry and why I have the audacity to call some people *dummies*.

Now, before we dig into the details of an *IUL*, I hope you understand that the title of this book (and the title of this first chapter) is a bit *tongue-in-cheek*, and I hope you have enough sense of self-deprecating humor to realize this. The reality is, unless you are a product technician and *math nerd* like I am, you are in fact a *dummy* in this particular area – the area of life insurance product design. And if you are an aspiring *know-it-all*, this book will teach you practically everything you need to know about an *IUL*.

All jesting aside, the remaining contents of this book are very serious and are intended to educate and deepen your understanding of how, when, and why using an *IUL* for your family's estate plan (as well as your own retirement) can be so valuable.

Once you fully understand the how/why/when components of this financial instrument, you will gain a much greater level of confidence when making financial decisions regarding life insurance that will impact you and your family.

If you are a client that is considering using an *IUL* as a retirement planning tool, or if you are a financial advisor, CPA, estate planning attorney, or life insurance agent that wants to gain a deeper understanding of how an *IUL* actually works, this is the right book for you.

In the next chapter, we will begin by discussing the preferential tax treatment that *IULs* receive, and why wealthy people LOVE life insurance.

Chapter 2
Wealthy People

Wealthy people LOVE life insurance, and for good reason. The three most common ways wealthy people use life insurance policies are to:

1. Provide liquidity to fund lifestyle expenses for their family in the event of a pre-mature death.
2. Generate a tax-free supplemental retirement income.
3. Pay the 40% in estate taxes due when wealth is transferred to the next generation (assuming their net worth would warrant this taxation).

Wealthy people typically want a conservative alternative to a *taxable bonds portfolio*, and the 0% floor of an *IUL* provides that conservative alternative. In addition, the tax-free cash value accumulation inside a life insurance policy is also very appealing to wealthy people.

But the appeal doesn't stop there. They also like the fact that the retirement income drawdowns from the policy can be tax-free as well. I have an entire chapter in this book devoted to explaining the different ways to take these tax-free income drawdowns *(Chapter 5: Policy Drawdowns)*. This benefit can even be enjoyed by non-wealthy people that own an *IUL*.

In addition, when a wealthy individual passes away, their assets can be passed on to their surviving spouse without tax consequence, however once their surviving spouse passes away and their wealth is transferred to the next generation, their heirs may incur a substantial tax liability in the form of *estate taxes* (currently 40%) depending on the estate's value at such time, and depending on the *Estate Tax Exemption Limit* at such time.

The IRS allows a certain amount of their net worth to be transferred to the next generation tax-free up until a certain dollar amount known as the *Estate Tax Exemption Limit*.

This exemption has increased each year since 2017. Below, we see these increases since 2017 (sourced from *https://www.irs.gov/pub/irs-pdf/i706.pdf*):

2017: $5,490,000 ($10,980,000 per married couple)
2018: $11,180,000 ($22,360,000 per married couple)
2019: $11,400,000 ($22,800,000 per married couple)
2020: $11,580,000 ($23,160,000 per married couple)
2021: $11,700,000 ($23,400,000 per married couple)
2022: $12,060,000 ($24,120,000 per married couple)
2023: $12,920,000 ($25,840,000 per married couple)

This year in 2024, this exemption limit has increased again.

2024: $13,610,000 ($27,220,000 per married couple)

Upon death, a spouse can pass their exemption on to their surviving spouse. However what many feared regarding the *Biden Administration's* tax agenda came to pass on September 13, 2021 when the *House Ways and Means Committee* released a tax change proposal in favor of reducing the estate tax exemption limit back down to the $5,000,000 range per individual in 2026.

However, one thing that has remained constant is the favorable tax treatment of life insurance, which is why it continues to be an incredibly valuable estate planning tool.

Due to *Section 101a* of the IRS tax code, the death benefit of a life insurance policy is tax-free, giving policy owners a huge advantage when the policy is owned in an *Irrevocable Life Insurance Trust (ILIT)* outside their taxable estate, despite their net worth being far above the thresholds I mentioned earlier.

If however, the client's estate is worth less than the thresholds I mentioned earlier (including the death benefit of the policy), the policy can be individually owned inside their estate and the death benefit is tax-free as well.

I will discuss comparing life insurance strategies to non-insurance-based alternatives later in this book, however it is important to understand that when a person dies, any excess net worth above the estate tax exemption is currently taxed at a rate of

40.00% when it is transferred to the next generation. The creates a substantial tax liability for *Generation Two (G2)*.

To clarify how this works, when one spouse passes away, the surviving spouse does not incur any estate tax liability. However when the second spouse dies and the estate is transferred to the next generation, estate taxes are incurred by the inheriting generation.

As an example, if the surviving spouse is worth $100,000,000 above the exemption limit, at the time of their passing, the inheriting generation will owe $40,000,000 in estate taxes (40.00% of the $100,000,000). This inheriting generation is only given nine months from the time of their surviving parent's death to file and pay the estate taxes due, which is not much lead time by any means.

Even if the estate value is comprised of illiquid assets (e.g., real estate, a company, jewelry, art, automobile collection, etc.), the estate tax is still due on the value of these assets nonetheless, which often results in a necessary *fire sale* of such assets to come up with the funds required to pay the estate taxes. This can be both financially and emotionally draining for all parties involved.

Life insurance is an extremely efficient tool in planning for the estate tax liability that the next generation will incur because it removes the need to liquidate the estate's illiquid assets within this nine-month period.

If the policy is owned by an *Irrevocable Life Insurance Trust (ILIT)* – which is outside the taxable estate – the death benefit will pay out tax-free to the *ILIT* and is not subject to estate taxes. The *ILIT* can then pay the estate taxes due once the death benefit is issued. This is a much easier process to manage than a desperate *fire sale* of illiquid assets just to come up with the cash needed to pay the estate taxes.

When it comes to estate tax planning, wealthy clients essentially have two options:

1. Do nothing and give away 40% of their wealth to the government in the form of estate taxes, or…

2. Use life insurance to pay the estate taxes for them.

Making the decision to buy life insurance should be based on one simple mathematical equation:

If the money you would have spent on life insurance can be invested in an alternative asset, and that asset value (after 40.00% estate taxes) becomes greater than the tax-free death benefit of the life insurance policy, then you should NOT buy the life insurance policy. But if 60% of that alternative asset value is less valuable than the net death benefit, then you SHOULD buy the life insurance. It really is that simple.

There is certainly an emotionally-driven population that feels like they are leaving enough assets behind for *Generation Two (G2)* and don't feel the need to purchase life insurance. Perhaps they have even said, *"No one ever left me an inheritance. My kids are lucky to get whatever I leave them."*

The reality is, wealthy parents are either going to leave the money to their kids, a charity, or *Uncle Sam*. Even if they don't want to make their kids overly wealthy, I have yet to meet a wealthy individual that prefers the IRS over their favorite charity.

The problem that many wealthy families face is that if the majority of the estate's value is *not* liquid (e.g. real estate value, business valuation, etc.), *Generation Two (G2)* would have to sell the estate's assets to come up with the cash to pay the estate taxes due, and they only have nine months to make this payment.

The IRS does however have an option to finance the estate taxes due. According to IRC Section 6166, *G2* may defer payment of estate taxes if 35%+ of the deceased person's estate is a closely held business. *G2* can pay interest-only in years 1-5 on the estate taxes due, then they can pay principle plus interest amortized over years 6-15. If *G2* defaults on this IRS loan, the IRS can seize and sell the asset.

An advisor once told me about one of his clients wherein the estate was worth $114,000,000 at the time of the second parent's death in 2006. At that time, the estate tax exemption for a married couple was only $4,000,000 (instead of the current $27,220,000 per couple in 2024) and the estate tax rate was 46% (instead of the current 40%). The family's business was in the real estate industry. *G2* elected the 6166 option because they didn't have the liquidity to pay the $50 million in estate taxes due.

Two years later in 2008, the estate/business value plummeted from $114,000,000 to only $54,000,000. *G2's* income plummeted as well, and they defaulted on the 6166 loan.

The IRS seized the estate's assets and sold them for their new fair market value of $54,000,000. However this reduction in estate valuation did not affect the $50,000,000 in estate taxes still due. You see, the estate taxes were calculated based on the value of the estate at the time of death, regardless of the plummeted value two years later.

Ultimately, *G2* was left with only $4,000,000 after they inherited a $114 million estate from their parents.

In this scenario, had there been a $50,000,000 life insurance policy in an *ILIT* (*Irrevocable Life Insurance Trust*) outside the estate to pay the future estate tax liability, *G2* could have inherited the entire estate, undiluted by estate taxes. Over time, the family's real estate values and business valuation would have recovered.

In addition, when wealthy parents pass away, it can drive huge wedges between siblings if the estate plan is not well designed and/or clearly delineated. When siblings argue over who gets to keep certain sentimental assets (like the family home and the family business), versus what assets need to be sold in order to pay the estate taxes, it can absolutely destroy a family.

This is why providing liquidity in their time of need is so important, and typically, life insurance – specifically *Premium Financed Life Insurance* – is the most prudent and tax-efficient way to provide such liquidity.

Though it is clearly important to understand the client's financial position when developing an estate plan, the single-most important thing for an advisor to understand is how to identify the difference between what a client *says* they want today, versus how they will *feel* in the future if their personal financial situation does not meet their aspirations.

This can be a challenging truth to uncover – one that takes a tremendous amount of psychological, sociological, and emotional intuitiveness on behalf of the advisor. It also takes a high level of understanding the inter-family relationship dynamics and family governance (or lack thereof).

Here's an example to illustrate what I mean by this.

Let's say you have a wealthy family with a taxable estate value of $100 million. When the patriarch and matriarch both pass away, as of 2024, their heirs will owe $40 million in estate taxes within nine months of their passing. If the majority of the estate value is held in illiquid assets (e.g., Real Estate, Company Valuation, etc.), the adult kids will be forced to sell assets to come up with the cash to pay the 40% in estate taxes.

In this hypothetical example, the eldest son is running the family business and does not want to sell any shares of the business to pay the estate taxes – the family business is his *baby*. The youngest son is living on the family yacht in Miami, living the *playboy* lifestyle, and certainly doesn't want to sell the yacht and the penthouse to pay the estate taxes. The daughter is resentful that she was not chosen to run the family business, and she has a sentimental attachment to the family vacation house in the Hamptons where they spent their summers growing up, and she doesn't want to sell it to pay the estate taxes. Of course, each respective sibling could care less about the assets their other siblings care about, and these disagreements over which assets to liquidate in order to pay the $40 million in estate taxes can absolutely destroy the relationships between siblings.

If there are spouses, children, and grandchildren involved, this can make these family disputes even more volatile. You see, it's not *just* the financial elements that are important. The emotional/relationship dynamics are also important – perhaps even more important.

This is where a properly structured life insurance policy can be such a valuable tool in regards to estate planning and family governance. Assets can be split amongst the surviving siblings based on their preference and emotional attachments, and the life insurance death benefit can take care of the estate taxes due, keeping the peace.

When people ask me what I do for a living, I now say, *"When wealth is transferred from one generation to the next, I make sure the adult kids don't kill each other."*

This response often times leads to some pretty interesting cocktail party discussions without me even trying to solicit my services. You would be amazed that despite how much I try to avoid talking about what I do for a living in social settings, people are fascinated by this topic of inter-family relationship dynamics, especially amongst uber-wealthy families.

There are many benefits of using life insurance as both an estate tax planning tool, as well as a tax-advantaged asset for wealth accumulation and supplemental retirement income. Even if your net worth is not at the level wherein your heirs would be subject to estate taxes, life insurance can still be a valuable asset for you to own.

But this is an industry wherein the explanations of how these insurance-based instruments actually work is *opaque* at best. One of the biggest criticisms of the life insurance industry is that many of the products lack transparency, and quite frankly, I would have to agree with that accusation… sort of, but not completely.

The reality is that many of these life insurance products do not lack transparency in their *construction*. The lack of transparency is in how their construction is *communicated* to the client – both from the carriers and the agents. It is a problem I experienced as a life insurance *client* back before I got into this line of work, and it is a problem that still exists today.

The key is to understand how different types of life insurance policies are built and how they work mechanically. This is the foundation I built my practice on. Everything I do is rooted in education and granular understanding.

In this book, I will open up the *black box* so you can see what's actually inside the box, which will change your perspective from looking through *opaque lenses* to looking through a *high-powered microscope*. The strong stance I have taken on opening up this *black box* has at times felt like I was opening *Pandora's Box*, but as I stated earlier, I am an industry disruptor – a beacon of transparency – and my goal is to teach you the truth about these products, where the risks are, how to mitigate these risks, and to show you the best way to utilize these products in the most effective way possible.

If you are not familiar with the details of the Greek mythological story of *Pandora's Box*, indulge me for just a moment to share with you how analogous this story is to *Indexed Universal Life Insurance (IUL)*.

In Greek mythology, *Pandora* was the first woman on Earth. She was given a box that the gods told her contained special gifts, but she was also told that she was not allowed to open it and see what was inside.

Eventually, *Pandora* could not contain her curiosity and she opened the box. When she did, all the illnesses and hardships that the gods had hidden in the box started coming out. She tried to close the box once she saw the evil coming out of it, but in doing so, *hope* got trapped inside the box.

Many people feel the same way about certain life insurance products. They are told that the *black box* contains all kinds of special gifts (e.g., tax-free benefits, 0% floor, etc.), but they are told not to open the box and dissect its components at the granular level. In fact, I've even heard advisors say, *"My clients don't want to know all the details."*

Personally, I think that statement greatly underestimates the curiosity of high-net worth clients. To say that a person worth $100 million doesn't want to understand how an *IUL* works is an incredibly naïve thing to say, and from my own personal experience, a very inaccurate thing to say.

So far, I have only talked about why *wealthy* people love life insurance. But perhaps you are not worth $100 million. What if your net worth is far below this amount. In fact, what if your net worth is less than $1 million, and you make less than $100,000 per year? Is an *IUL* still an effective financial tool you should have in your retirement portfolio?

Each person's unique circumstance would dictate my answer to this question, however ask yourself these questions:

1. If you were die unexpectedly early, your family would no longer have your income to pay the bills (mortgage, car payments, etc.). Could they maintain their lifestyle and pay for living expenses without your income? If the answer is *no*, perhaps you need some life insurance coverage.

2. Do you think income taxes are going to go up or down? If you think taxes are going up in the future, perhaps you might enjoy the tax-free retirement income an *IUL* could provide you with.

3. Are you concerned about market crashes during your retirement years? If you are, perhaps you might enjoy the 0% protective floor than an *IUL* provides.

4. When you die, do you want your adult kids to fight over which assets to sell and which assets to keep? If the answer is *no*, you might want to use life insurance to provide the liquidity needed so your kids don't kill each other fighting over assets.

When I started teaching advisors and their clients how *IULs* work at the granular level, my result was much different than *Pandora's* because when I opened up the *black box* of *IULs*, not only did the evils of the life insurance industry come out, but so did *hope*. Sure, I exposed certain products and their design flaws, but I have also been able to uncover the truth about how a well-designed *IUL* can be one of the most valuable assets in legacy planning AND retirement planning that exists – assuming it is designed properly and used with the right client.

Before I knew anything about life insurance, my financial advisor lost me $930,000 in three years due to a poorly designed life insurance strategy. I'm still not certain whether or not he was aware of what he was doing when he designed that strategy.

If he was *aware*, he was commission-greedy and unethical.

If he was *unaware*, then he was irresponsible and incompetent.

Either way, I was the one got hurt financially.

The purpose of this book is to teach you how these products actually work – specifically the *Indexed Universal Life Insurance (IUL)* product – so that you fully understand not only the general concept, but the granular details as well.

WARNING

The next five chapters are going to be highly technical and granular in detail. These chapters are perfect for *Aspiring Know-It-Alls*, *Insurance Geeks*, and *Math Nerds*. If you are one of these aforementioned types of people, then you are *my* kind of people. You want to know the truth about how these products are built and how they function in the real world.

I love people that are constantly seeking the truth. I also love math, because the math doesn't lie. It doesn't care about how you *feel*. It only cares about the truth.

The next five chapters will explain policy charges, floors and caps, income drawdowns, multiplier bonuses, and how my backtesting software can model the sustainability of an *IUL* construction during times of volatility.

If you do NOT want to learn the details about how this product is constructed and you want to keep it simple, you may skip to **Chapter 8: My Own IUL** which explains why I personally own an *IUL* and **Chapter 9: About The Author** where I share my background and the history of my experience in the life insurance industry.

If however you are an *Aspiring Know-It-All*, you are going to love these next five chapters. I will begin by uncovering the truth about *IUL* policy charges.

Chapter 3
Policy Charges

When most financial professionals measure risk, they typically have conversations about *Standard Deviation, Sharpe Ratios*, and *Monte Carlo* simulations.

These risk-measuring techniques are certainly important topics of discussion because they address the *Probability Of Risk*, however they all fail to articulate the most important element of risk: *The Consequence Of Risk*.

I was once asked if my proprietary backtesting software ran *Monte Carlo* simulations. I understood the spirit of their question, however I explained that *Monte Carlo* simulations merely measure the *Probability Of Risk*. So I asked him what level of risk he was comfortable with. 80% probability of a positive outcome? 90% probability of a positive outcome?

The gentleman told me he was comfortable with a 90% probability of a positive outcome (10% probability of a negative outcome).

I said, *"Okay, if I put ten hand guns on the table, and NINE of them have no bullets in them, but ONE of the ten has a bullet in the chamber, how comfortable are you picking up one of the guns, putting it to your head, and squeezing the trigger?"*

His comfort level with 90% probability of a positive outcome quickly faded. In this scenario, the *Probability Of Risk* was relatively low, however the *Consequence Of Risk* was extremely high.

When it comes to life insurance, I measure both the *Probability Of Risk* and the *Consequence Of Risk*.

Though I am not a CPA or tax attorney (which means that I cannot give tax advice or legal advice), I can mathematically model different *IUL* strategies, compare them to non-insurance-based solutions, and showcase different financial outcomes using certain tax assumptions. I can also model certain unfavorable assumptions that put extra strains on the *IUL* proposition, which I think is vitally important to model for clients in the spirit of full transparency and proper due diligence.

This industry lacks full client disclosure, so being the *beacon of transparency* – albeit a self-proclaimed title – is the main reason I am the trusted source of $20 million to $100 million *Premium Financed Life Insurance* policy designs and strategies for top advisors, producer groups, CPAs, tax attorneys, family offices, and carriers in the life insurance industry.

If the spirit of advisor/client conversations is rooted in education, consumer protection, and risk mitigation, then the foundation of these conversations will be client-centric, which is what they should be. My goal in all communication efforts is to transparently articulate how the math works, and if the indisputable math tells us that one particular *IUL* is the most advantageous to the client compared to other viable alternatives in an array of backtested scenarios (I analyze 121 different historical 40-year periods), the decision to move forward with that particular design is an obvious one. I have devoted an entire chapter to explaining how my backtesting software works *(Chapter 7: Backtesting)*.

Conversely, there have even been scenarios where my mathematical modeling process proved that it was *not* in the client's best interest to use an *IUL*, and in such scenarios, I am the first one to discourage them from moving forward. Some advisors don't like that I'm so blunt with my recommendations against *IULs* in these scenarios, and some of them will even try to get me to rework the numbers to favor the *IUL* proposition. In these rare instances, my answer is always the same: *The math either works, or it doesn't work. The math doesn't lie.*

Remember, I'm the guy that won't even sugarcoat a cookie.

Your journey in understanding the true *Consequence Of Risk* in poorly designed *IUL* policies starts with understanding how policy charges and credits actually work.

When a carrier receives the policy premium for an *IUL* product, the first charge that is deducted is the *Premium Load*. Assuming the premium is paid annually at the *Beginning Of The*

Year (BOY), the *Premium Loads* are also deducted at the *BOY*. The remaining policy charges (e.g., Cost of Insurance, Administration Fees, Mortality Expenses, etc.) are then deducted monthly.

Assuming the client selected a *1-Year Annual Point-To-Point* index option, the *segment* begins in the month the premium is swept into the index account (e.g., the 15th day of the month), and ends twelve months later. At the end of this 12-month segment, the index credit is then determined based on the underlying index's performance during that 1-year segment wherein the *IUL's* cap and floor would be applied to the gross accumulated value of the policy (not the *net* cash surrender value, but the *gross* accumulated value). Some carriers apply this index credit to the *EOY Accumulated Value (EOYAV)*, whereas other carriers apply the index return to the *Average Monthly Accumulated Value (AMAV)*.

Mathematically speaking, the *AMAV* is a higher number than the *EOYAV* because it does not account for 100% of the monthly charges. In other words, in the second month of the segment, only 2/12 of the monthly charges have been deducted, hence the accumulated value in that month would be higher than the accumulated value in the eleventh month wherein 11/12 of the monthly charges were deducted.

For the sake of this discussion, we will assume that the *Indexed Universal Life (IUL)* insurance product applies the index credit to the *EOY Accumulated Value*. We will also assume that the product's underlying index tracks the S&P 500's performance, with a 0.00% floor and a 9.00% cap. In the event that the S&P 500 produced a positive return of 15.00% in a given year, the policy index credit would credit 9.00%, not exceeding the maximum allowable return (the cap).

	$1,000,000	Previous Year's EOY Accumulated Value
+	$0	New Policy Premium
	$1,000,000	**Current Year's BOY Accumulated Value**
-	$50,000	Current Year's Policy Charges
	$950,000	**Current Year's EOY Accumulated Value (Before Index Credit)**
x	9.00%	Index Credit (assuming a +15.00% S&P 500 Return & 9.00% cap)
	$85,000	**Accumulated Index Credit (Accumulated Value Gain)**
+	$950,000	Current Year's EOY Accumulated Value (Before Index Credit)
	$1,035,500	**Current Year's EOY Accumulated Value (After Index Credit)**

However if the S&P 500 produced a negative return in a given year, the index credit would be 0.00% (the floor). This stop-loss feature of this particular crediting method acts as a risk-mitigation tool, which is certainly one of the most valuable elements of the *IUL* product chassis.

However, one of the most inaccurate statements I've heard some life insurance agents say is, *"With the IUL's 0.00% floor, you can never lose money."* Mathematically speaking, this is not a true statement. It is true that you would not receive a negative index return (an index return less than the 0.00% floor), however that is only true AFTER the policy charges have been deducted from the policy value. If the policy charges were $50,000 in a given year, and the *BOY* cash surrender value was $1,000,000 (assuming a 0.00% index credit in such year), the *EOY* cash surrender value would be $950,000.

```
      $1,000,000  Previous Year's EOY Accumulated Value
+             $0  New Policy Premium
      $1,000,000  Current Year's BOY Accumulated Value
-        $50,000  Current Year's Policy Charges
        $950,000  Current Year's EOY Accumulated Value (Before Index Credit)
x          0.00%  Index Credit (assuming a -15.00% S&P 500 Return & 0.00% floor)
              $0  Accumulated Index Credit (Accumulated Value Gain)
+       $950,000  Current Year's EOY Accumulated Value (Before Index Credit)
        $950,000  Current Year's EOY Accumulated Value (After Index Credit)
```

In this example, the policy's *Accumulated Value* would have actually decreased by $50,000 despite the 0.00% floor.

The first risk factor to understand in an *IUL* is the relationship between *policy index credits* and *policy charges*.

One of the problems I have with clients making buying decisions solely based on standard carrier illustrations is that they depict a positive static index return every year with no simulations of volatility wherein 0.00% index returns are modeled (as they were in the example I just explained).

What this means is that the discussion (and mathematical modeling) of negative arbitrage during 0.00% return years is never properly articulated (and certainly never mathematically stress-tested) in most advisor/client discussions.

As I mentioned earlier in this book, one of the main things that makes me stand apart from other life insurance specialists is my ability to mathematically model scenarios wherein these design elements (e.g., floors, caps, charges, etc.) can be modeled during times of volatility so you can actually see the potential effects of these different variables.

I will discuss how my backtesting software has the ability to model these variables (and their effects on potential outcomes) later in this book.

But first, let's discuss how the floors and caps are created by the carriers, as well as the long-term sustainability of such product features.

Chapter 4
Floors & Caps

The 0.00% floor sounds too good to be true, doesn't it?

Years ago when I first heard about this *IUL* feature, I thought the same thing. Most people do not truly understand how this feature actually works, and this seemingly mysterious *black box* makes intelligent people skeptical (as they should be). I am still shocked that the life insurance industry does not do a better job of explaining how the *floor & cap proposition* mechanically works in practice, because once you understand it, you will appreciate just how well thought out (and how sustainable) this design element truly is.

To understand how an *IUL*'s crediting method works, we must first discuss the origin of permanent life insurance policies in general. We will start with one type of permanent life insurance policy: *Whole Life*.

Whole Life is not synonymous with the category of ALL permanent life insurance policies. *Whole Life* is one of several different types of permanent life insurance. Compared to *Term* life insurance (which expires after the term period), *Whole Life* was originally designed to give a person life insurance coverage that would last for their whole/entire life, hence the name *Whole Life*.

The general concept was that the premiums (approximately four times greater than *Term* insurance premiums) would not only pay for the cost of insurance, but the excess premiums would be *invested* in the life insurance company itself (somewhat similar to buying stock in the insurance company – not exactly, but similar). These excess premiums invested in the life insurance company would yield a *dividend* based on how well the life insurance company's overall investment portfolio did in the previous year.

A dividend would be declared, then it would be credited to the policy's cash value the following year. The cash value would then be used to pay for the ongoing *Cost Of Insurance* (long after the insured person stopped paying premiums) which enabled the policy to last until the end of the insured person's life – insuring them for their *whole* life. To give you an idea of how stable these *Whole Life* dividends have been over time, below are the historical dividend credits over the last forty years of four major *Whole Life* carriers.

YEAR	CALENDAR YEAR	GUARDIAN DIVIDENDS	MASS MUTUAL DIVIDENDS	NORTHWESTERN DIVIDENDS	PENN MUTUAL DIVIDENDS	LOWEST DIVIDEND OF 4 CARRIERS
1	1983	7.65%	8.27%	9.75%	6.58%	6.58%
2	1984	12.25%	11.60%	10.75%	7.15%	7.15%
3	1985	13.25%	12.20%	11.00%	11.20%	11.00%
4	1986	13.25%	12.20%	11.25%	11.20%	11.20%
5	1987	12.50%	12.20%	11.00%	8.20%	8.20%
6	1988	12.00%	11.35%	10.25%	8.20%	8.20%
7	1989	11.50%	11.15%	10.00%	9.93%	9.93%
8	1990	11.00%	10.50%	10.00%	9.93%	9.93%
9	1991	10.50%	10.50%	10.00%	9.93%	9.93%
10	1992	10.25%	9.95%	9.25%	9.93%	9.25%
11	1993	9.75%	9.45%	9.25%	9.70%	9.25%
12	1994	9.00%	9.30%	8.50%	9.20%	8.50%
13	1995	8.50%	9.00%	8.50%	8.50%	8.50%
14	1996	8.00%	8.40%	8.50%	8.50%	8.00%
15	1997	8.50%	8.40%	8.50%	8.00%	8.00%
16	1998	8.75%	8.40%	8.80%	8.00%	8.00%
17	1999	8.75%	8.40%	8.80%	7.40%	7.40%
18	2000	8.50%	8.30%	8.80%	7.40%	7.40%
19	2001	8.50%	8.30%	8.80%	7.40%	7.40%
20	2002	8.00%	8.10%	8.60%	7.40%	7.40%
21	2003	7.00%	7.90%	8.20%	6.48%	6.48%
22	2004	6.60%	7.50%	7.70%	5.74%	5.74%
23	2005	6.75%	7.00%	7.50%	5.74%	5.74%
24	2006	6.50%	7.55%	7.50%	6.30%	6.30%
25	2007	6.75%	7.55%	7.50%	6.30%	6.30%
26	2008	7.25%	7.90%	7.50%	6.34%	6.34%
27	2009	7.30%	7.45%	6.50%	6.34%	6.34%
28	2010	7.00%	6.85%	6.15%	6.34%	6.15%
29	2011	6.85%	6.80%	6.00%	6.34%	6.00%
30	2012	6.95%	7.00%	5.85%	6.34%	5.85%
31	2013	6.65%	7.00%	5.60%	6.34%	5.60%
32	2014	6.25%	7.10%	5.60%	6.34%	5.60%
33	2015	6.05%	7.10%	5.60%	6.34%	5.60%
34	2016	6.05%	7.10%	5.45%	6.34%	5.45%
35	2017	5.85%	6.70%	5.00%	6.34%	5.00%
36	2018	5.85%	6.70%	5.00%	6.34%	5.00%
37	2019	5.85%	6.40%	5.00%	6.10%	5.00%
38	2020	5.65%	6.20%	6.20%	6.10%	5.65%
39	2021	5.65%	6.00%	6.00%	5.75%	5.65%
40	2022	5.65%	6.00%	5.00%	5.75%	5.00%
	AVERAGE:	8.22%	8.39%	7.88%	7.44%	7.15%

In addition, most *Whole Life* products also guarantee a minimum annual return (typically around 4.00%).

One of the main benefits of the cash value accumulation inside a life insurance policy is tax-free growth (due to IRS tax code 7702). This favorable tax treatment eventually led to the category of *permanent life insurance* expanding into several additional products with more aggressive underlying investments.

When *Variable Universal Life (VUL)* insurance products hit the market, the idea was to use mutual funds as the underlying investments instead of the life insurance carrier's guaranteed return and dividend crediting method. In concept, the client could use the same mutual funds they were already investing in, but by housing them inside a life insurance construct, the gains on these mutual funds would be tax-free.

It was a great concept in theory, especially when mutual fund returns were sky-high like they were in the mid-80's and 90's. But when the tech bubble burst in the early 2000's, it was a rude awakening for *VULs* because in order to offset the high policy expenses that were built into the *VUL* construction, the underlying mutual fund returns needed to perform as they did in the previous two decades. When this did not happen during *The Lost Decade* (2000-2009 wherein the S&P 500 produced several negative returns during this ten-year run), these expense *charges* began to outpace the *VULs' credits*. Today, many advisors and consumers have shifted their interest away from *VUL* policies towards *IUL* policies.

Unlike a *VUL* policy that can experience negative returns, *IULs* have a *floor* – a minimum index credit – which is typically 0.00%. The question is, *"How is this possible and how is this sustainable?"*

If you recall, the *Whole Life* product crediting method included a guaranteed return plus a dividend based on how profitable the life insurance company was in the previous year. In an *IUL* product, the carrier essentially takes the guaranteed return they were going to automatically credit in the *Whole Life* policy and uses that amount as the budget to purchase *options contracts*.

I am going to attempt to explain the general mechanics of how this works without getting too overly detailed, for the full explanation would require a 1,000+ page book. In my attempt to teach you the basics, I will articulate this as succinctly as possible. Additionally, in the spirit of full disclosure, there are details that vary from carrier to carrier, product to product.

For example, *Allianz* does not currently use investment banking firms to purchase their options contracts. They do it in-house due to the massive amount of options purchasing they do to support both their *IUL* products and their *Indexed Annuities*, so their method of utilizing S&P 500-correlated options contracts is different. I am not saying the *Allianz's IUL* products are necessarily better or worse than other carriers' *IULs*. I am just mentioning their unique way of buying options.

As another example of differentiation, *Pacific Life* applies their index credit to the *Average Monthly Accumulated Value*, whereas most other carriers apply their index credit to the *EOY Accumulated Value*, which is a lower value. Again, I am not saying that *Pacific Life's IUL* products are necessarily better or worse than other carriers' *IULs*. I am just mentioning their unique way calculating their index crediting method.

These are just two of many examples of how each product from each carrier is built slightly differently, however learning about *IULs* in general is best done by using one hypothetical example.

In this hypothetical example, the carrier purchases *options* from an investment banking firm – S&P 500-correlated options with a 0.00% floor. The budget for this type of arrangement is approximately 4.00% of the life insurance premium ($4,000 per $100,000 in insurance premium). But remember, that was the amount the carrier was going to automatically credit the *Whole Life* policy's cash value anyway, so in this scenario, the carrier has zero exposure because that allocation was already built into the pricing.

The investment banking firm takes the $4,000 as the *options premium*, and if the S&P 500 produces a negative return, they absorb the losses and pass the benefit of the 0.00% floor on to the carrier, who then passes the benefit on to the policy. Though the investment banking firm absorbs the loss below 0.00%, they do get to keep the $4,000 options premium.

If the S&P 500 produces a positive return, they pass that return through to the carrier, who then passes the return through to the policy, up to a maximum allowable return (the cap), and any return above the cap is then retained by the investment banking firm in addition to the $4,000 options premium per $100,000 in insurance premium.

The carrier does not incur any risk in a negative S&P 500 return scenario, and they do not participate in any of the upside above the cap either. Remember, the $4,000 options premium they paid the investment banking firm was already budgeted into the contract pricing, so for the policy owner, the decision to buy an *IUL* instead of a *Whole Life* policy is based on the belief that over time, the returns of the S&P 500-correlated index fund with a floor and cap with outpace the dividend returns of a *Whole Life* product.

This decision could be based on the client analyzing historical S&P 500 performance using the floor and cap assumptions, and comparing them to historical *Whole Life* dividend returns.

This decision could also be influenced by the conservative nature of the *Whole Life* dividend crediting history which has never produced a 0.00% return, let alone a negative return.

However, there are several elements in addition to the dividend or index return that also determine the actual cash value yield over time.

For example, policy charges need to be factored into the equation. The actual sequence of returns that a policy experiences also plays a major role in accumulation.

Another variable that affects cash value accumulation is the method in which retirement income drawdowns are taken from the policy values.

The following chart shows historical S&P 500 returns and different floors and caps. Again, merely comparing average *Whole Life* dividends to average S&P 500-correlated *after-floor/after-cap* returns does not tell the entire story.

YEAR	CALENDAR YEAR	S&P 500 RETURNS (NO DIVIDENDS)	9.00% CAP 0.00% FLOOR	10.00% CAP 0.00% FLOOR	11.00% CAP 0.00% FLOOR	12.00% CAP 0.00% FLOOR
1	1983	17.26%	9.00%	10.00%	11.00%	12.00%
2	1984	1.38%	1.38%	1.38%	1.38%	1.38%
3	1985	26.36%	9.00%	10.00%	11.00%	12.00%
4	1986	14.62%	9.00%	10.00%	11.00%	12.00%
5	1987	2.04%	2.04%	2.04%	2.04%	2.04%
6	1988	12.39%	9.00%	10.00%	11.00%	12.00%
7	1989	27.25%	9.00%	10.00%	11.00%	12.00%
8	1990	-6.56%	0.00%	0.00%	0.00%	0.00%
9	1991	26.30%	9.00%	10.00%	11.00%	12.00%
10	1992	4.48%	4.48%	4.48%	4.48%	4.48%
11	1993	7.07%	7.07%	7.07%	7.07%	7.07%
12	1994	-1.56%	0.00%	0.00%	0.00%	0.00%
13	1995	34.13%	9.00%	10.00%	11.00%	12.00%
14	1996	20.26%	9.00%	10.00%	11.00%	12.00%
15	1997	31.01%	9.00%	10.00%	11.00%	12.00%
16	1998	26.67%	9.00%	10.00%	11.00%	12.00%
17	1999	19.53%	9.00%	10.00%	11.00%	12.00%
18	2000	-10.14%	0.00%	0.00%	0.00%	0.00%
19	2001	-13.04%	0.00%	0.00%	0.00%	0.00%
20	2002	-23.37%	0.00%	0.00%	0.00%	0.00%
21	2003	26.38%	9.00%	10.00%	11.00%	12.00%
22	2004	8.99%	8.99%	8.99%	8.99%	8.99%
23	2005	3.00%	3.00%	3.00%	3.00%	3.00%
24	2006	13.60%	9.00%	10.00%	11.00%	12.00%
25	2007	3.52%	3.52%	3.52%	3.52%	3.52%
26	2008	-38.49%	0.00%	0.00%	0.00%	0.00%
27	2009	23.65%	9.00%	10.00%	11.00%	12.00%
28	2010	12.63%	9.00%	10.00%	11.00%	12.00%
29	2011	0.10%	0.10%	0.10%	0.10%	0.10%
30	2012	13.29%	9.00%	10.00%	11.00%	12.00%
31	2013	29.43%	9.00%	10.00%	11.00%	12.00%
32	2014	11.54%	9.00%	10.00%	11.00%	11.54%
33	2015	-0.73%	0.00%	0.00%	0.00%	0.00%
34	2016	9.54%	9.00%	9.54%	9.54%	9.54%
35	2017	19.42%	9.00%	10.00%	11.00%	12.00%
36	2018	-6.24%	0.00%	0.00%	0.00%	0.00%
37	2019	28.88%	9.00%	10.00%	11.00%	12.00%
38	2020	16.26%	9.00%	10.00%	11.00%	12.00%
39	2021	26.89%	9.00%	10.00%	11.00%	12.00%
40	2022	-19.44%	0.00%	0.00%	0.00%	0.00%
Average Returns:		**9.96%**	**5.94%**	**6.50%**	**7.05%**	**7.59%**

What I find mildly fascinating is that when comparing the average index credits seen above (during this particular historical 40-year period) to the average *Whole Life* dividend credits shown during the same historical 40-year period (as depicted a few pages ago), the average *Whole Life* dividend credits from three of the four carriers I analyzed are better than the average *IUL's* S&P 500-correlated *after-floor/after-cap* credits, even with a 12.00% cap. However, the *after-floor/after-cap* credits in this chart do not include any bonuses that may exist in some real world *IULs*, including both *persistency bonuses* and *multiplier bonuses* (which I will discuss later in this book).

But merely comparing the average historical *Whole Life* dividend credits to the historical *IUL* index credits does not give you a complete picture of which is *better*.

The reason I say this is that retirement income drawdowns from the policy cash value can be done in three different ways in an *IUL*.

1. Withdrawals.
2. Fixed Loans.
3. Participating Loans.

Some *Whole Life* products will not allow the policy owner to drawdown policy values as efficiently as *IUL* products, and when using a cash value life insurance policy as a retirement income vehicle, this is an extremely important attribute to consider when attempting to maximize retirement income drawdowns from the policy AND for the long-term sustainability of the policy.

Yes, some *Non-Direct Recognition Whole Life* carriers allow drawdowns to be taken in a similar fashion to the way *Participating Loans* are treated in an *IUL* (currently *New York Life* and *Mass Mutual* allow this), while other *Direct Recognition Whole Life* carriers limit the drawdowns to be treated similarly to *Fixed Loans* in an *IUL*.

In the next chapter, I will explain the difference between *Withdrawals*, *Fixed Loans*, and *Participating Loans* in an *IUL*.

Chapter 5
Policy Drawdowns

There are three ways to take drawdowns from an *IUL* when generating supplemental retirement income. You can take *Withdrawals*, *Fixed Policy Loans*, or *Participating Policy Loans*.

1. Withdrawal.

In a *withdrawal* scenario, the drawdown amount is literally withdrawn from the *Gross Accumulated Cash Value*. From that moment forward, the remaining *Net Accumulated Value* of the policy receives the annual *after-floor/after-cap* index credit each year.

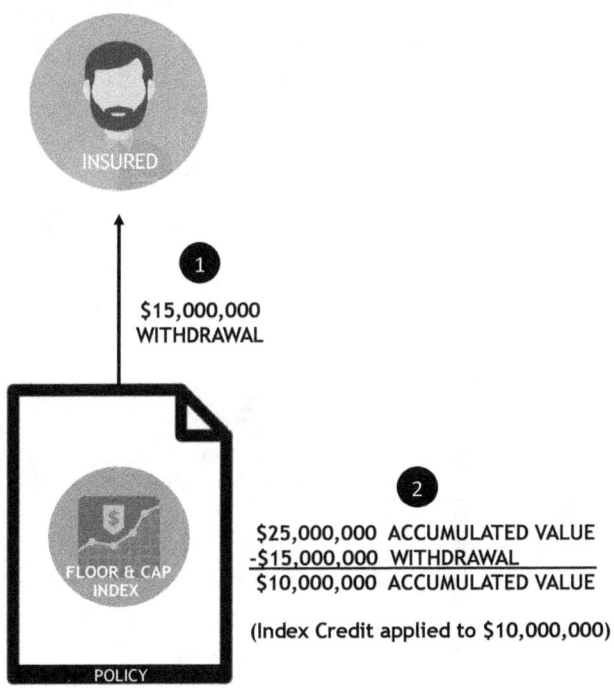

2. Fixed Loan (AKA "Wash Loan").

When taking a *Fixed Policy Loan*, the drawdown amount is removed from the policy *Gross Accumulated Cash Value* and placed into a separate account that credits a fixed return (3.00% as a hypothetical example) instead of the annual *after-floor/after-cap* index credit each year. The carrier then "loans" the policy owner the same drawdown amount and "charges" interest on the policy loan at the same interest rate the fixed account credits (3.00% in this example), making it a *wash loan*. Similar to the *Withdrawal* scenario, from that moment forward, only the remaining *Net Accumulated Cash Value* of the policy receives the annual *after-floor/after-cap* index credit each year.

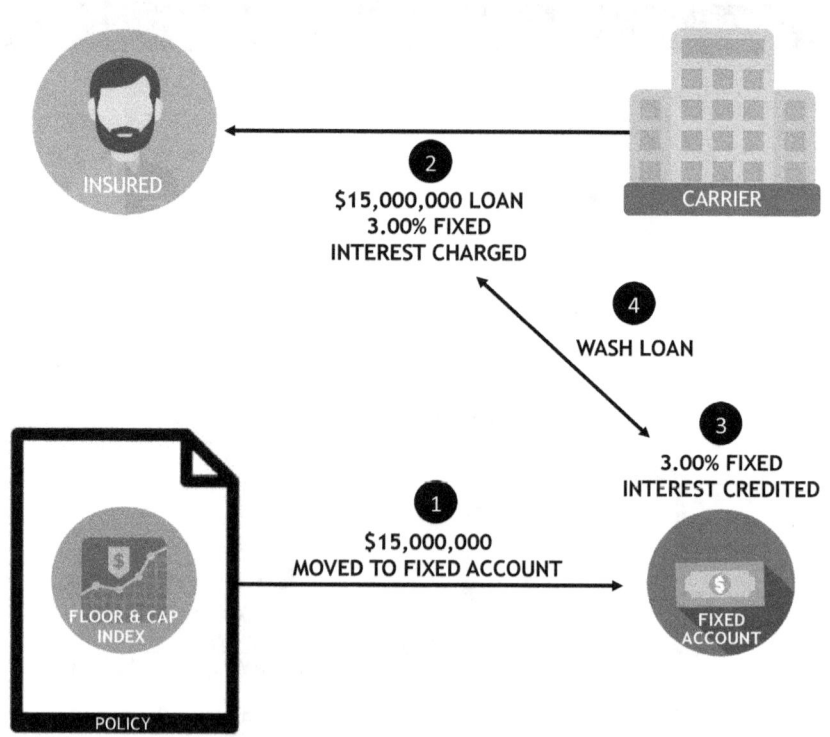

3. Participating Loan (AKA "Indexed Loan").

When taking a *Participating Policy Loan*, with some carriers, the drawdown amount is removed from the *Gross Accumulated Cash Value* and placed into a separate index account that receives the same (or similar) annual *after-floor/after-cap* index credit as the policy's *Cash Value*. With other carriers, the drawdown amount actually remains in the policy's *Gross Accumulated Cash Value*. The carrier then "loans" the policy owner the same drawdown amount and "charges" interest on this policy loan. Sometimes the interest rate charged is a fixed amount (5.00% for example), and sometimes the interest rate is a variable floating rate. In this policy loan strategy, the policy owner is hoping the *S&P 500-correlated floor & cap* index crediting method will outpace the *Participating Loan* interest charged.

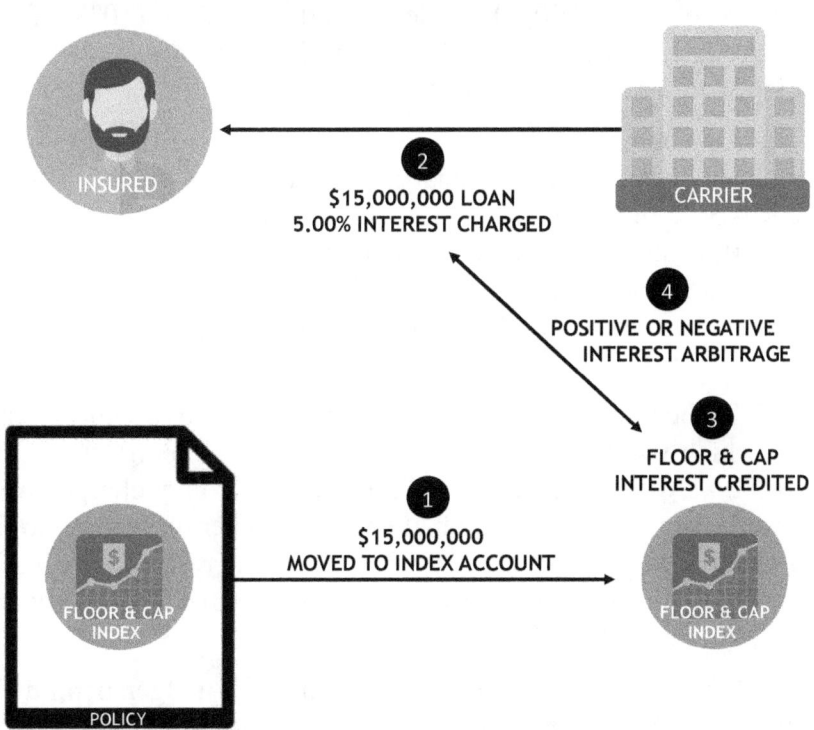

The anticipated benefit of the *Participating Loan* is that from the moment the *Participating Loan* is taken, the annual *after-floor/after-cap* index credit is applied to the *Gross Accumulated Value* in the policy, not the *Net Accumulated Value*. If the funds were moved into a separate index account (supposing the carrier of choice uses this method), these funds are also credited based on the *after-floor/after-cap* index credit methodology.

This is perhaps the most misunderstood (and undervalued) component of an *IUL*. The fact that the annual index credit is applied to the *Gross Accumulated Value* (not the *Net Value*) means that as the index credit is applied to the larger *gross* value.

As an example, if the *IUL* had a *Gross Accumulated Value* of $1,000,000 in a given year (after charges) and a cumulative *Participating Loan* amount of $700,000 (due to retirement income drawdowns), the *Net Cash Value* would be $300,000.

If the *IUL's* index credit in that year was 10%, the policy would receive a $100,000 index credit that year (10% of the $1,000,000 cash value), not 10% of the $300,000 *Net Cash Value* (which would only be $30,000).

Of course, that would be partially offset by the *Participating Loan* interest charged, so if the *Participating Loan* rate was 5%, the $700,000 *Participating Loan* amount would result in $35,000 interest charged in that given year, making the *Net Policy Cash Value* increase by $65,000 in that year ($100,000 index credit minus $35,000 interest charged equals $65,000 net gain).

To be fair, if the S&P 500 produced a negative return in that year (which would have resulted in a 0% index credit), the *IUL's Cash Value* would receive zero gains after the policy charges were deducted from the cash value that year. However in addition to the charges, the $35,000 in *Participating Loan* interest would also be subtracted from the *Net Cash Value* (not the *Gross Accumulated Value*, but the *Net Cash Value*).

The accounting of this is all done on a ledger behind the scenes with the carrier, making it easy for the policy owner. In other words, the policy owner does not need to do any independent accounting to manage the interest charged and credited.

To evaluate the risk of *Participating Loans* and the potential negative arbitrage between the loan interest charged and the 0% index credited in given years, my backtesting software analyzes 121 different historical 40-year periods of S&P 500 performance, builds a *proxy* for the *IUL* with the *Participating Loan* component, and models the 40-year period that produced the *Worst Compounded Annual Growth Rate* of the 121 different historical 40-year periods, for this is the type of scenario wherein the *Participating Loan* proposition might incur a negative outcome.

During the challenging 40-year sequence, we evaluate the relationship between the *Participating Loan* interest accrued versus the gains made by keeping the payoff amount in the policy's *Gross Accumulated Value* (or separate index account if the carrier uses such methodology). Over such time, if the debt outpaces the growth on such *Participating Loan* funds, it would be prudent for the client to make their decisions based on whether or not they want to incur that risk, despite how much more profitable such proposition may be during better index performing times. I always provide this analytical report to my clients and review it with them.

If the 40-year period that produced the *Worst Compounded Annual Growth Rate* of the 121 different historical 40-year periods shows a net gain in such *Participating Loan* proposition, that stress-test becomes just as valuable in the client's overall education and awareness.

To be clear, this evaluation model is not a modified version of an *IUL* illustration. That would violate *AG-49A* guidelines and several other compliance regulations. I created a *Hypothetical Synthetic Asset* – a fictitious index account – that behaves very similar to an *IUL* in regards to charges, crediting methodology, and participating loan methodology.

The goal is to see how these factors could potentially affect short-term and long-term outcomes during times of volatility. For example, in certain sequences of returns we analyze, there are several consecutive 0.00% index credits within the first ten years of the 40-year sequence.

In other scenarios we model, the consecutive 0.00% index returns happen in the middle of the 40-year sequence during the beginning years of income drawdowns which puts excessive stress on cash value accumulation which is needed to keep the policy in force.

In an effort to be extremely clear in this discussion, the scenario that I called *"the 40-year period that produced the Worst Compounded Annual Growth Rate of the 121 different historical 40-year periods analyzed"* is not the worst possible 40-year outcome imaginable. It is just the worst one of the 121 different periods I analyzed. It is within the realm of possibility that the next forty years could be even worse than the *Worst 40-Year Period* out of these 121 periods I analyzed, just as it is possible that the next forty years could produce an even better outcome than the *Best 40-Year Period* I analyzed.

Perhaps this overly granular explanation is painfully redundant, however I believe it is important to communicate in a crystal clear manner so it is virtually impossible to misinterpret my mathematical findings.

Before we delve into my backtesting methodology, in this next chapter, I will address one of the most controversial topics of discussion when it comes to *IULs*: *Multiplier Bonuses & Asset-Based Charges.*

Chapter 6
Multiplier Bonuses

One of the most controversial design elements in modern-day *IULs* is the *Multiplier Bonus*. At the moment, the majority of *IUL* multiplier propositions allow a client to accept an additional asset-based charge in exchange for a multiplier bonus that enhances the index return. In this arrangement, the client *doubles down* on the carrier's ability to buy more options contracts from the investment bankers. Often times, *IUL* critics accuse *IUL Multipliers* of being opaque, mysterious, and expensive, however the multiplier proposition is actually quite simple.

As an example, if the multiplier bonus factor is 1.45X, this means that the *after-floor/after-cap* index return would be multiplied by 1.45, giving the pre-multiplier return a 45.00% boost. In this example there is a maximum return allowable of 2.15% above the cap. 9.00% x 1.45 = 13.05%, however the maximum return allowable in this given year is 9.00% + 2.15% = 11.15%.

```
      15.00%  End-Of-Segment S&P 500 Return
  >    9.00%  Hypothetical IUL Cap
       9.00%  End-Of-Segment After-Floor/After-Cap Return
  x    1.45   Multiplier Bonus
      13.05%  After Bonus (this does not include the 2.15% max above cap)
      11.15%  EOY Index Credit After Multiplier Bonus
```

If the client likes this proposition, they can elect to purchase this feature each year at policy renewal for an asset-based charge. For example, if the asset-based multiplier charge is 1.00%, that means the policy receives an additional charge on top of the standard policy charges, calculated by multiplying 1.00% by the *Accumulated Value* and deducted from the *Accumulated Value* in the current year (1/12 of 1.00%, monthly).

Pre-*AG-49A*, one of the biggest criticisms of these multiplier features was that the carrier illustration depicted a static positive index credit each year, which illustrated a multiplier advantage each year. In other words, if the carrier illustration showed a static 5.50% index return every year, and the multiplier bonus factor was 1.45X, the illustration's cash value growth in the illustration was actually calculated based on a 7.98% index credit (5.50% x 1.45 = 7.98%), not the stated 5.50%.

Using the static positive index credits in a carrier's illustration was misleading because in a real-world scenario, the S&P 500 is going to experience some negative return years wherein the policy's index credit would be 0.00%. In these years, not only would the policy's cash value decrease due to the standard policy charges, but the additional 1.00% multiplier asset-based charge would create an additional reduction in cash value.

The *IUL* multiplier critics and die-hard *Whole Life* fans accused *IUL* illustrations of being misleading because the illustrations assumed a positive multiplier bonus each year, not taking into consideration the substantial reduction in cash value the additional asset-based charges could cause during 0.00% index crediting years, and they were right... sort of.

The problem was that no one did the math.

The critics were making broad conceptual assertions that the multiplier propositions were too risky and the asset-based charges too costly, but they had no mathematically-proven analytics to back up their claims.

On the other side of the fence were the over-zealous *IUL* fanatics that reveled in showing the massively bolstered returns and claimed that *IUL*s with multiplier bonuses were the best thing since sliced bread, but they had no mathematically-proven analytics to back up their claims either.

So who was right? Neither of them.

As a result, the regulators passed a new actuarial guideline – *AG-49A* – that restricted carrier illustrations from illustrating multiplier bonuses. The illustrations could now only show multiplier asset-based charges, but no multiplier bonuses. The non-sensical nature of this restriction didn't solve the problem they were trying to solve.

I would agree that an illustration that depicts a positive static return every year wherein a multiplier bonus enhances the index return *every year* tells a very incomplete and inaccurate story of how multiplier *IULs* actually work, but I would also say that showing a carrier illustration with multiplier asset-based charges with no multiplier bonus credits also tells a very inaccurate story.

As a result of the illogical way this restriction was implemented, most agents started running illustrations *without* any multiplier features. The problem with this decision was that if the client intended to buy an *IUL* with a multiplier feature, the agent was showing the client something they were not actually going to buy. This is perhaps the most inaccurate scenario of all scenarios an agent could present to a client.

To complicate things even further, if the client was actually going to buy an *IUL* with a multiplier feature, and they were originally shown an illustration without the multiplier feature, just prior to policy delivery, the client had to sign a version of the illustration that included all the product features they were actually buying, which included the multiplier feature. This meant that the agent had to re-run the illustration and include the multiplier asset-based charges, which then depicted a much worse cash value accumulation outcome because the additional charges eroded the as-illustrated *Cash Value* with no multiplier bonus enhancement taken into consideration. This version of the illustration looked substantially worse than the first version the client saw when they initially made their decision to buy, which made the agent look like they had *bait-and-switched* the offering.

As an alternative, the agent could have just started off showing the client a version of the illustration that included all of the multiplier charges (but did not include any of the multiplier benefits), and say, *"Trust me, there are multiplier bonuses included, but I can't show them in the carrier illustration."*

That would be like trying to sell a *$550,000 Lamborghini Aventador* that actually puts out 770 horsepower, despite the brochure stating that it only puts out 570 horsepower, and telling the client, *"Trust me, not the brochure."*

The third option the agent had was to not sell any *IULs* with multiplier bonus features whatsoever, restricting the client from

41

buying something that might be tremendously beneficial to their overall estate plan, retirement plan, and overall financial plan. Clearly, this was not a good option either.

I am a big supporter of compliance and industry regulation in general, for I believe the spirit of *regulated compliance* is rooted in consumer protection, and consumer protection is a good thing.

But *AG-49A* did not solve the problem of *lack of transparency* in carrier illustrations. It just exchanged one problem for another – exchanging one inaccurate depiction for another inaccurate depiction. The illustrative limitations and inaccuracies that *AG-49A* created didn't stop there either.

AG-49A also required the carrier illustration to depict a static *Participating Loan Rate* equal to 0.50% less than the index crediting rate illustrated, despite what the actual *Participating Loan Rate* was. In other words, if the carrier illustration assumed a 5.75% index crediting rate, the *Participating Loan Rate* had to be illustrated at 5.25%, even if the actual *Participating Loan Rate* was only 5.00%.

This problem was two-fold.

First, this depiction showed a *Participating Loan Rate* that was not accurate. And second, because the illustration depicted a positive static index credit every year, there was always a positive arbitrage between the index credit and the *Participating Loan Rate*, which will not happen in years when the actual *Index Credit* is lower than the actual *Participating Loan Rate*.

In a year wherein the *Participating Loan Rate* was 5.00% and the index credit was 2.00%, the client would actually lose 3.00% in that negative arbitrage year (2.00% - 5.00% = -3.00%). However if the *Participating Loan Rate* was 5.00%, and the index credit was 9.00%, the client would actually gain 4.00% in that positive arbitrage year (9.00% - 5.00% = 4.00%).

Being as conservative as I am in regards to not wanting a client to buy an unrealistically positive depiction of what the *IUL* can do, I must say that the *AG-49* restrictions put on carrier illustrations are rather emasculating. In my humble opinion, they lead a client to believe something that is unreasonably negative.

Think about this for a moment.

The maximum allowable index credit a carrier can show in their illustration is the average of every 25-year window over the most recent 65 years. This scenario depicts the 50th percentile, meaning that the index credit assumption assumes that the IUL has a 50% chance of failing.

In most consumer buying scenarios, we don't make our decision to buy (or not buy) based on assuming the product we're buying has a 50% chance of failure.

Would you buy a car with seatbelts that have a 50% failure rate? Would you even buy a computer that says in their product brochure that it has a 50% chance of failure? Of course not.

I am certainly NOT saying that the client shouldn't see a scenario wherein there is a 50% of failure. I think it is logical to show this assumption as ONE of several potential outcomes. I also think it would be logical to show ONE scenario that is even *worse* that this, as well as another scenario wherein an even *better* outcome is modeled. But to call it the *Maximum Index Credit* the carrier can illustrate .

This is why my backtesting software's capabilities are so valuable, because they can mathematically articulate both types of scenarios in each given year so the client can actually see how the math works during times of volatility. I will explain these capabilities in the next chapter.

Chapter 7
Backtesting

So far, I have discussed the problems I see with the assumptions and limitations depicted in carrier illustrations, as well as how *IUL* crediting and charges methods actually work in real-world scenarios. In this chapter, I will explore how floors, caps, multipliers and asset-based charges can impact financial outcomes. I will do so by reviewing a case study using data sourced directly from an actual premium financed *IUL* policy, but I will do so by analyzing the behavior of a *Hypothetical Synthetic Asset* that will act as a proxy for an *IUL* (hereinafter called *The Proxy*).

When I started developing my proprietary backtesting software over a decade ago, I had no idea it would evolve into what it is today. Its capabilities of deconstructing an *IUL's* chassis, measuring risk during times of volatility, and testing the efficacy of different product designs is truly unparalleled.

As I stated earlier in this book, my process begins with analyzing 121 different historical 40-year periods. I use one-year annual point-to-point segments and track them over 40-year rolling periods.

The first 40-year period I analyzed started on January 1, 1970 and tracked historical S&P 500 performance for the next forty years (forty 12-month segments), ending on December 31, 2009. The second 40-year period I analyzed started one month later on February 1, 1970 and ended on January 31, 2010. The third one started one month after that on March 1, 1970 and ended on February 28, 2010. These 40-year sequences continued with the 121st one starting on January 1, 1980 and ending on December 31, 2019.

In the spirit of conservatism (and arguably pessimism), I will focus on the 40-year period that produced the *Worst Compounded Annual Growth Rate* of all the 121 different 40-year periods analyzed. To be clear, this particular 40-year period was only the "worst" one based on the *Compounded Annual Growth*

Rates of the 121 different 40-year periods I analyzed, not the *"worst possible case scenario that could ever exist in the future."*

It is certainly possible that the next forty years could produce an even worse *Compounded Annual Growth Rate* than this sequence, and it is also possible that the next forty years could

4 BACKTESTED YEAR	5 INDEX GROSS RETURN	6 INDEX CREDIT		7 MULTIPLIER BONUS (x)		8 INDEX CREDIT w/ MULTIPLIER		9 PERSISTENCY BONUS (+)		10 TOTAL INDEX CREDIT (%)
1971	12.42%	10.00%	x	1.00	=	10.00%	+	0.00%	=	10.00%
1972	-1.92%	0.00%	x	1.28	=	0.00%	+	0.00%	=	0.00%
1973	-41.40%	0.00%	x	1.37	=	0.00%	+	0.00%	=	0.00%
1974	32.00%	10.00%	x	1.46	=	14.60%	+	0.00%	=	14.60%
1975	25.48%	10.00%	x	1.55	=	15.50%	+	0.00%	=	15.50%
1976	-8.28%	0.00%	x	1.64	=	0.00%	+	0.00%	=	0.00%
1977	6.23%	6.23%	x	1.73	=	10.77%	+	0.00%	=	10.77%
1978	6.61%	6.61%	x	1.82	=	12.03%	+	0.00%	=	12.03%
1979	14.76%	10.00%	x	1.91	=	19.10%	+	0.00%	=	19.10%
1980	-7.40%	0.00%	x	1.91	=	0.00%	+	0.00%	=	0.00%
1981	3.65%	3.65%	x	1.91	=	6.97%	+	0.00%	=	6.97%
1982	37.91%	10.00%	x	1.91	=	19.10%	+	0.00%	=	19.10%
1983	0.02%	0.02%	x	1.91	=	0.03%	+	0.00%	=	0.03%
1984	9.62%	9.62%	x	1.91	=	18.38%	+	0.00%	=	18.38%
1985	27.04%	10.00%	x	1.91	=	19.10%	+	0.00%	=	19.10%
1986	39.13%	10.00%	x	1.91	=	19.10%	+	0.00%	=	19.10%
1987	-15.51%	0.00%	x	1.91	=	0.00%	+	0.00%	=	0.00%
1988	28.41%	10.00%	x	1.91	=	19.10%	+	0.00%	=	19.10%
1989	-12.34%	0.00%	x	1.91	=	0.00%	+	0.00%	=	0.00%
1990	26.73%	10.00%	x	1.91	=	19.10%	+	0.00%	=	19.10%
1991	7.72%	7.72%	x	1.81	=	13.97%	+	0.00%	=	13.97%
1992	9.84%	9.84%	x	1.70	=	16.74%	+	0.00%	=	16.74%
1993	0.82%	0.82%	x	1.59	=	1.31%	+	0.00%	=	1.31%
1994	26.30%	10.00%	x	1.48	=	14.80%	+	0.00%	=	14.80%
1995	17.61%	10.00%	x	1.37	=	13.70%	+	0.00%	=	13.70%
1996	37.82%	10.00%	x	1.37	=	13.70%	+	0.00%	=	13.70%
1997	7.36%	7.36%	x	1.37	=	10.08%	+	0.00%	=	10.08%
1998	26.13%	10.00%	x	1.37	=	13.70%	+	0.00%	=	13.70%
1999	11.99%	10.00%	x	1.37	=	13.70%	+	0.00%	=	13.70%
2000	-27.54%	0.00%	x	1.37	=	0.00%	+	0.00%	=	0.00%
2001	-21.68%	0.00%	x	1.37	=	0.00%	+	0.00%	=	0.00%
2002	22.16%	10.00%	x	1.37	=	13.70%	+	0.00%	=	13.70%
2003	11.91%	10.00%	x	1.37	=	13.70%	+	0.00%	=	13.70%
2004	10.25%	10.00%	x	1.37	=	13.70%	+	0.00%	=	13.70%
2005	8.71%	8.71%	x	1.37	=	11.93%	+	0.00%	=	11.93%
2006	14.29%	10.00%	x	1.37	=	13.70%	+	0.00%	=	13.70%
2007	-23.61%	0.00%	x	1.37	=	0.00%	+	0.00%	=	0.00%
2008	-9.37%	0.00%	x	1.37	=	0.00%	+	0.00%	=	0.00%
2009	7.96%	7.96%	x	1.37	=	10.90%	+	0.00%	=	10.90%
2010	-0.86%	0.00%	x	1.37	=	0.00%	+	0.00%	=	0.00%

produce an even better *Compounded Annual Growth Rate* than the *Best 40-Year Period* of the 121 different 40-year periods I analyzed.

This particular 40-year historical period analyzed in this chart started on October 1, 1971 (column 4) and produced the *Worst Compounded Annual Growth Rate* of all the 121 different 40-year periods analyzed. These historical S&P 500 returns do not include S&P 500 dividends (column 5), and I am modeling a 10.00% hypothetical pre-multiplier cap (column 6). I am also modeling a multiplier bonus that ranges from 1.28X up to 1.91X in different years (column 7), with asset-based multiplier charges (I will explain how this asset-based charge works later in this chapter). The multiplier bonus was then accounted for in the *Index Credit w/ Multiplier* (column 8) which is the *after-floor/after-cap/after-multiplier* return.

In a year wherein the index return hits the 10.00% cap, the *Index Credit w/ Multiplier* can be as high as 19.10% in some years (10.00% x 1.91 = 19.10%) due to this multiplier bonus.

Some policies have a *Persistency Bonus* (column 9) which is then added to the *Index Credit w/ Multiplier* return, which equals the *Total Index Credit* (column 10). In this particular product modeled on the previous page, there is no *Persistency Bonus*.

It is important to note that in the first ten years of this 40-year sequence, the S&P 500 produced several negative returns, resulting in several 0.00% *Effective Index Returns* (an extremely poor sequence of returns).

Because the *The Proxy* depicted here is not a life insurance illustration (it is just a proxy for an *IUL*), there is no death benefit shown, for this is not a life insurance policy. However, because we are using the same fee structure as the charges in an actual *IUL* policy, as well as the same crediting structure as an actual IUL, the behavior of this *The Proxy* gives us some perspective regarding how an *IUL's Cash Value* might behave during the various 40-year sequences analyzed. This is a valuable depiction to consider because the charges and crediting methods used cause the ongoing net performance to behave very similar to an actual *IUL* product.

The reason this *Proxy* modeling is so important – even in a death benefit-focused case – is that a real world *IUL's* long-term sustainability is largely based on its *Cash Value's* ability to pay the future insurance charges AND outpace any compounding *Participating Loan* debt balance with the carrier that may exist from policy drawdowns to fund retirement income (or to pay off any premium financing loan debt if the policy was financed).

This particular graph below is included in all of my client proposals. It compares the net *Cash Surrender Value* as-illustrated in the carrier illustration (*thin solid line*) to the simulated net account values in *The Proxy* during the 40-year period with the *Best Compounded Annual Growth Rate* (*heavily dashed line*) and during the 40-year period with the *Worst Compounded Annual Growth Rate* (*dotted line*).

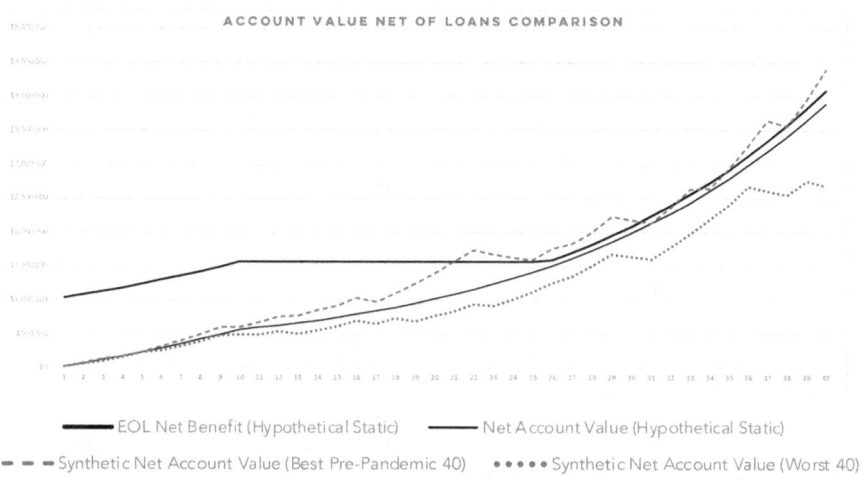

The real value of this graph is for the client to see there is a potential range of outcomes when it comes to the simulated cash value of *The Proxy*.

We also see by the sixth year, the account value of *The Proxy* during the best 40-year period (*bold dashed line*) not only pulls ahead of the as-illustrated *Cash Surrender Value* (*thin solid line*), but starting in year twenty-two, it also eclipses the carrier as-illustrated *Net Death Benefit* (*bold solid line*), and in many years between years 22-40, it continues to show a greater value.

If the *Net Cash Surrender Value* in a real world *IUL* equaled values depicted in the *bold dashed line*, the actual *Net Death Benefit* (*bold solid line*) would have to be greater than the *dashed line* because the *Net Death Benefit* in a real world *IUL* cannot be less than the policy's *Net Cash Surrender Value*.

In addition, *The Proxy* also transparently shows both the standard charges (using the same charge amounts in the carrier illustration) as well as the additional asset-based multiplier charges and compares the total charges to the total index credits each year (depicted in the next two pages).

# YEAR	AGE	1 ASSET-BASED CHARGES (%)	2 ASSET-BASED CHARGES ($)	3 FIXED CHARGES ($)	4 BACKTESTED YEAR	5 INDEX GROSS RETURN	6 INDEX CREDIT		7 MULTIPLIER BONUS (x)		8 INDEX CREDIT w/MULTIPLIER		9 PERSISTENCY BONUS (+)
1	50	0.00%	$0	-$9,534	1971	12.42%	10.00%	x	1.00	=	10.00%	+	0.00%
2	51	1.00%	-$864	-$10,131	1972	-1.92%	0.00%	x	1.23	=	0.00%	+	0.00%
3	52	1.50%	-$1,878	-$10,689	1973	-41.40%	0.00%	x	1.37	=	0.00%	+	0.00%
4	53	2.00%	-$3,247	-$11,214	1974	32.00%	10.00%	x	1.46	=	14.60%	+	0.00%
5	54	2.50%	-$5,512	-$11,737	1975	25.48%	10.00%	x	1.55	=	15.50%	+	0.00%
6	55	2.99%	-$8,540	-$12,680	1976	-8.28%	0.00%	x	1.64	=	0.00%	+	0.00%
7	56	3.50%	-$10,993	-$13,316	1977	6.23%	6.23%	x	1.73	=	10.77%	+	0.00%
8	57	3.99%	-$14,830	-$14,025	1978	6.61%	6.61%	x	1.82	=	12.03%	+	0.00%
9	58	4.49%	-$19,526	-$14,834	1979	14.76%	10.00%	x	1.91	=	19.10%	+	0.00%
10	59	4.98%	-$26,322	-$15,724	1980	-7.40%	0.00%	x	1.91	=	0.00%	+	0.00%
11	60	4.98%	-$24,524	-$9,863	1981	3.65%	3.65%	x	1.91	=	6.97%	+	0.00%
12	61	4.98%	-$24,409	-$10,237	1982	37.91%	10.00%	x	1.91	=	19.10%	+	0.00%
13	62	4.98%	-$27,056	-$10,591	1983	0.02%	0.02%	x	1.91	=	0.03%	+	0.00%
14	63	4.98%	-$25,182	-$10,913	1984	9.62%	9.62%	x	1.91	=	18.38%	+	0.00%
15	64	4.98%	-$27,724	-$11,204	1985	27.04%	10.00%	x	1.91	=	19.10%	+	0.00%
16	65	4.98%	-$30,901	-$5,707	1986	39.13%	10.00%	x	1.91	=	19.10%	+	0.00%
17	66	4.98%	-$34,654	-$5,893	1987	-15.51%	0.00%	x	1.91	=	0.00%	+	0.00%
18	67	4.98%	-$32,631	-$6,049	1988	28.41%	10.00%	x	1.91	=	19.10%	+	0.00%
19	68	4.98%	-$36,595	-$6,171	1989	-12.34%	0.00%	x	1.91	=	0.00%	+	0.00%
20	69	4.98%	-$34,463	-$6,252	1990	26.73%	10.00%	x	1.91	=	19.10%	+	0.00%
21	70	4.38%	-$34,002	-$6,258	1991	7.72%	7.72%	x	1.81	=	13.97%	+	0.00%
22	71	3.78%	-$31,729	-$6,140	1992	9.84%	9.84%	x	1.70	=	16.74%	+	0.00%
23	72	3.18%	-$29,775	-$5,819	1993	0.82%	0.82%	x	1.59	=	1.31%	+	0.00%
24	73	2.58%	-$23,552	-$5,212	1994	26.30%	10.00%	x	1.48	=	14.80%	+	0.00%
25	74	1.98%	-$20,114	-$4,198	1995	17.61%	10.00%	x	1.37	=	13.70%	+	0.00%
26	75	1.98%	-$22,343	-$2,639	1996	37.82%	10.00%	x	1.37	=	13.70%	+	0.00%
27	76	1.98%	-$24,852	-$1,953	1997	7.36%	7.36%	x	1.37	=	10.08%	+	0.00%
28	77	1.98%	-$26,773	-$2,295	1998	26.13%	10.00%	x	1.37	=	13.70%	+	0.00%
29	78	1.98%	-$29,786	-$2,665	1999	11.99%	10.00%	x	1.37	=	13.70%	+	0.00%
30	79	1.98%	-$33,135	-$3,092	2000	-27.54%	0.00%	x	1.37	=	0.00%	+	0.00%
31	80	1.98%	-$32,413	-$3,582	2001	-21.68%	0.00%	x	1.37	=	0.00%	+	0.00%
32	81	1.98%	-$31,695	-$4,162	2002	22.16%	10.00%	x	1.37	=	13.70%	+	0.00%
33	82	1.98%	-$35,229	-$4,828	2003	11.91%	10.00%	x	1.37	=	13.70%	+	0.00%
34	83	1.98%	-$39,152	-$5,589	2004	10.25%	10.00%	x	1.37	=	13.70%	+	0.00%
35	84	1.98%	-$43,508	-$6,457	2005	8.71%	8.71%	x	1.37	=	11.93%	+	0.00%
36	85	1.98%	-$47,590	-$7,523	2006	14.29%	10.00%	x	1.37	=	13.70%	+	0.00%
37	86	1.98%	-$52,868	-$8,656	2007	-23.61%	0.00%	x	1.37	=	0.00%	+	0.00%
38	87	1.98%	-$51,637	-$9,951	2008	-9.37%	0.00%	x	1.37	=	0.00%	+	0.00%
39	88	1.98%	-$50,402	-$11,456	2009	7.96%	7.96%	x	1.37	=	10.90%	+	0.00%
40	89	1.98%	-$54,534	-$13,184	2010	-0.86%	0.00%	x	1.37	=	0.00%	+	0.00%
			-$1,104,938	-$322,423									

Column 11 shows what the index credits would have been in each year in dollar amounts. In years wherein the index credited 0.00%, the cash value would obviously receive a $0 credit.

Column 12 shows what the total charges would have been based on the as-illustrated charges shown in the carrier illustration, plus what any additional asset-based charges would have been based on the accumulated value during this particular backtested period.

Then, column 13 shows what the net gain-or-loss would have been – the combination of any index credits received, offset by the total charges in that given year. In the years wherein the S&P 500 produced a negative return and the *Effective Index Credit* was 0.00%, this *Charges+Credits+Bonuses Report* also shows the reduction in account value during these years (the negative values depicted during several years in column 13).

IUL FOR ASPIRING KNOW-IT-ALLS

10 TOTAL INDEX CREDIT (%)	11 TOTAL INDEX CREDITS ($)	12 TOTAL CHARGES ($)	13 YEAR-END GAIN/LOSS ($)	14 EOY VALUE AFTER CHARGES B4 CREDIT	15 EOY GROSS INDEX ACCUMULATED VALUE	16 EOY INDEX VALUE NET OF INT & EXT LOANS
10.00%	$4,047	($9,534)	($5,487)	$40,466	$44,513	$24,598
0.00%	$0	($10,995)	($10,995)	$83,517	$83,517	$65,485
0.00%	$0	($12,567)	($12,567)	$120,951	$120,951	$104,830
14.60%	$22,847	($14,461)	$8,387	$156,490	$179,337	$165,141
15.50%	$32,874	($17,249)	$15,625	$212,088	$244,962	$232,712
0.00%	$0	($21,220)	($21,220)	$273,742	$273,742	$263,466
10.77%	$32,252	($24,309)	$7,943	$299,433	$331,685	$323,411
12.03%	$42,459	($28,855)	$13,605	$352,830	$395,290	$389,039
19.10%	$78,488	($34,360)	$44,128	$410,930	$489,418	$485,218
0.00%	$0	($42,046)	($42,046)	$497,372	$497,372	$495,258
6.97%	$32,273	($34,387)	($2,114)	$462,985	$495,258	$495,258
19.10%	$87,977	($34,646)	$53,331	$460,612	$548,589	$548,589
0.03%	$176	($37,647)	($37,471)	$510,942	$511,118	$511,118
18.38%	$87,288	($36,095)	$51,193	$475,023	$562,311	$562,311
19.10%	$99,966	($38,928)	$61,038	$523,383	$623,349	$623,349
19.10%	$112,068	($36,608)	$75,460	$586,742	$698,809	$698,809
0.00%	$0	($40,547)	($40,547)	$658,262	$658,262	$658,262
19.10%	$118,340	($38,680)	$79,660	$619,582	$737,923	$737,923
0.00%	$0	($42,766)	($42,766)	$695,157	$695,157	$695,157
19.10%	$124,998	($40,715)	$84,283	$654,442	$779,440	$779,440
13.97%	$103,277	($40,260)	$63,017	$739,180	$842,457	$842,457
16.74%	$134,652	($37,869)	$96,783	$804,588	$939,240	$939,240
1.31%	$11,834	($35,594)	($23,760)	$903,646	$915,480	$915,480
14.80%	$131,234	($28,764)	$102,470	$886,716	$1,017,950	$1,017,950
13.70%	$136,128	($24,312)	$111,817	$993,638	$1,129,766	$1,129,766
13.70%	$151,355	($24,982)	$126,373	$1,104,784	$1,256,140	$1,256,140
10.08%	$123,974	($26,805)	$97,169	$1,229,334	$1,353,309	$1,353,309
13.70%	$181,421	($29,068)	$152,353	$1,324,241	$1,505,662	$1,505,662
13.70%	$201,830	($32,451)	$169,379	$1,473,211	$1,675,041	$1,675,041
0.00%	$0	($36,227)	($36,227)	$1,638,814	$1,638,814	$1,638,814
0.00%	$0	($35,995)	($35,995)	$1,602,819	$1,602,819	$1,602,819
13.70%	$214,674	($35,857)	$178,817	$1,566,962	$1,781,636	$1,781,636
13.70%	$238,596	($40,057)	$198,540	$1,741,579	$1,980,176	$1,980,176
13.70%	$265,155	($44,741)	$220,413	$1,935,435	$2,200,589	$2,200,589
11.93%	$256,653	($49,965)	$206,688	$2,150,624	$2,407,277	$2,407,277
13.70%	$322,247	($55,113)	$267,134	$2,352,165	$2,674,411	$2,674,411
0.00%	$0	($61,524)	($61,524)	$2,612,888	$2,612,888	$2,612,888
0.00%	$0	($61,588)	($61,588)	$2,551,300	$2,551,300	$2,551,300
10.90%	$271,403	($61,858)	$209,544	$2,489,442	$2,760,844	$2,760,844
0.00%	$0	($67,718)	($67,718)	$2,693,126	$2,693,126	$2,693,126
	$3,620,487	-$1,427,361	$2,193,126			

The Proxy's Charges+Credits+Bonuses Report uncovers a the truth about the multiplier proposition in this particular case study, especially during adverse market conditions. The *Asset-Based Charge* (column 1) in exchange for the *Multiplier Bonus* (column 7) is a proposition that is actually solid, assuming the *IUL* was constructed responsibly by both the carrier and the advisor. The advisor's knowledge and skillset in the area of policy design is vitally important. The same exact product can be *tuned* by the advisor properly (and improperly). As an example, you could own a *Ferrari*, but if you have a *dummy* mechanic that isn't an expert in exotic Italian sports cars, your *Ferrari* could blow up.

In *The Proxy*, the previous year's *EOY Gross Index Account Value* (column 15 of the previous year) minus 50% of the *Fixed Charges* is calculated (since the charges are monthly charges), then the *Asset-Based Charge* is applied to this value, equaling the *Asset-Based Charges ($)* in that given year (column 2).

51

# YEAR	AGE	1 ASSET-BASED CHARGES (%)	2 ASSET-BASED CHARGES ($)	3 FIXED CHARGES ($)	4 BACKTESTED YEAR	5 INDEX GROSS RETURN	6 INDEX CREDIT		7 MULTIPLIER BONUS (x)		8 INDEX CREDIT w/ MULTIPLIER		9 PERSISTENCY BONUS (+)
1	50	0.00%	$0	-$9,534	1971	12.42%	10.00%	x	1.00	=	10.00%	+	0.00%
2	51	1.00%	-$864	-$10,131	1972	-1.92%	0.00%	x	1.28	=	0.00%	+	0.00%
3	52	1.50%	-$1,878	-$10,689	1973	-41.40%	0.00%	x	1.37	=	0.00%	+	0.00%
4	53	2.00%	-$3,247	-$11,214	1974	32.00%	10.00%	x	1.46	=	14.60%	+	0.00%
5	54	2.50%	-$5,512	-$11,737	1975	25.48%	10.00%	x	1.55	=	15.50%	+	0.00%
6	55	2.99%	-$8,540	-$12,680	1976	-8.28%	0.00%	x	1.64	=	0.00%	+	0.00%
7	56	3.50%	-$10,993	-$13,316	1977	6.23%	6.23%	x	1.73	=	10.77%	+	0.00%
8	57	3.99%	-$14,830	-$14,025	1978	6.61%	6.61%	x	1.82	=	12.03%	+	0.00%
9	58	4.49%	-$19,526	-$14,834	1979	14.76%	10.00%	x	1.91	=	19.10%	+	0.00%
10	59	4.98%	-$26,322	-$15,724	1980	-7.40%	0.00%	x	1.91	=	0.00%	+	0.00%
11	60	4.98%	-$24,524	-$9,863	1981	3.65%	3.65%	x	1.91	=	6.97%	+	0.00%
12	61	4.98%	-$24,409	-$10,237	1982	37.91%	10.00%	x	1.91	=	19.10%	+	0.00%
13	62	4.98%	-$27,056	-$10,591	1983	0.02%	0.02%	x	1.91	=	0.03%	+	0.00%
14	63	4.98%	-$25,182	-$10,913	1984	9.62%	9.62%	x	1.91	=	18.38%	+	0.00%
15	64	4.98%	-$27,024	-$11,204	1985	27.04%	10.00%	x	1.91	=	19.10%	+	0.00%
16	65	4.98%	-$30,901	-$5,707	1986	39.13%	10.00%	x	1.91	=	19.10%	+	0.00%
17	66	4.98%	-$34,654	-$5,893	1987	-15.51%	0.00%	x	1.91	=	0.00%	+	0.00%
18	67	4.98%	-$32,631	-$6,049	1988	28.41%	10.00%	x	1.91	=	19.10%	+	0.00%
19	68	4.98%	-$36,595	-$6,171	1989	-12.34%	0.00%	x	1.91	=	0.00%	+	0.00%
20	69	4.98%	-$34,463	-$6,252	1990	26.73%	10.00%	x	1.91	=	19.10%	+	0.00%
21	70	4.38%	-$34,002	-$6,258	1991	7.72%	7.72%	x	1.81	=	13.97%	+	0.00%
22	71	3.78%	-$31,729	-$6,140	1992	9.84%	9.84%	x	1.70	=	16.74%	+	0.00%
23	72	3.18%	-$29,775	-$5,819	1993	0.82%	0.82%	x	1.59	=	1.31%	+	0.00%
24	73	2.58%	-$23,552	-$5,212	1994	26.30%	10.00%	x	1.48	=	14.80%	+	0.00%
25	74	1.98%	-$20,114	-$4,198	1995	17.61%	10.00%	x	1.37	=	13.70%	+	0.00%
26	75	1.98%	-$22,343	-$2,639	1996	37.82%	10.00%	x	1.37	=	13.70%	+	0.00%
27	76	1.98%	-$24,852	-$1,953	1997	7.36%	7.36%	x	1.37	=	10.08%	+	0.00%
28	77	1.98%	-$26,773	-$2,295	1998	26.13%	10.00%	x	1.37	=	13.70%	+	0.00%
29	78	1.98%	-$29,786	-$2,665	1999	11.99%	10.00%	x	1.37	=	13.70%	+	0.00%
30	79	1.98%	-$33,135	-$3,092	2000	-27.54%	0.00%	x	1.37	=	0.00%	+	0.00%
31	80	1.98%	-$32,413	-$3,582	2001	-21.68%	0.00%	x	1.37	=	0.00%	+	0.00%
32	81	1.98%	-$31,695	-$4,162	2002	22.16%	10.00%	x	1.37	=	13.70%	+	0.00%
33	82	1.98%	-$35,229	-$4,828	2003	11.91%	10.00%	x	1.37	=	13.70%	+	0.00%
34	83	1.98%	-$39,152	-$5,589	2004	10.25%	10.00%	x	1.37	=	13.70%	+	0.00%
35	84	1.98%	-$43,508	-$6,457	2005	8.71%	8.71%	x	1.37	=	11.93%	+	0.00%
36	85	1.98%	-$47,590	-$7,523	2006	14.29%	10.00%	x	1.37	=	13.70%	+	0.00%
37	86	1.98%	-$52,868	-$8,656	2007	-23.61%	0.00%	x	1.37	=	0.00%	+	0.00%
38	87	1.98%	-$51,637	-$9,951	2008	-9.37%	0.00%	x	1.37	=	0.00%	+	0.00%
39	88	1.98%	-$50,402	-$11,456	2009	7.96%	7.96%	x	1.37	=	10.90%	+	0.00%
40	89	1.98%	-$54,534	-$13,184	2010	-0.86%	0.00%	x	1.37	=	0.00%	+	0.00%
			-$1,104,938	-$322,423									

To make it easier for you to reference my commentary, this is the same ledger as shown in the previous two pages.

Regarding the substantial multiplier charges (column 2), the multi-million dollar question is, *"Are they worth it?"* Though the *Asset-Based Charges* (column 2) are significant, during the worst 40-year period, column 13 answers this question. The 0.00% return years show the *Year-End Losses* in column 13, however relative to the *Year-End Gains* in this same column, the gains drastically outweigh the *Asset-Based Charges* that come with the multiplier bonuses. Let's discuss how the multiplier bonus works. Column 5 shows the historical S&P 500 returns each year. The floor and cap are applied, creating the *Pre-Multiplier Index Credit* (column 6), which is then multiplied by the *Multiplier Bonus* (column 7) totaling the *Index Credit w/ Multiplier* (column 8). In some real world *IUL*s, there is an additional persistency bonus (column 9).

In this example, there is no such bonus. The *Total Index*

10 TOTAL INDEX CREDIT (%)	11 TOTAL INDEX CREDITS ($)	12 TOTAL CHARGES ($)	13 YEAR-END GAIN/LOSS ($)	14 EOY VALUE AFTER CHARGES B4 CREDIT	15 EOY GROSS INDEX ACCUMULATED VALUE	16 EOY INDEX VALUE NET OF INT & EXT LOANS
10.00%	$4,047	($9,534)	($5,487)	$40,466	$44,513	$24,598
0.00%	$0	($10,995)	($10,995)	$83,517	$83,517	$65,485
0.00%	$0	($12,567)	($12,567)	$120,951	$120,951	$104,830
14.60%	$22,847	($14,461)	$8,387	$156,490	$179,337	$165,141
15.50%	$32,874	($17,249)	$15,625	$212,088	$244,962	$232,712
0.00%	$0	($21,220)	($21,220)	$273,742	$273,742	$263,466
10.77%	$32,252	($24,309)	$7,943	$299,433	$331,685	$323,411
12.03%	$42,459	($28,855)	$13,605	$352,830	$395,290	$389,039
19.10%	$78,488	($34,360)	$44,128	$410,930	$489,418	$485,218
0.00%	$0	($42,046)	($42,046)	$497,372	$497,372	**$495,258**
6.97%	$32,273	($34,367)	($2,114)	$462,985	$495,258	$495,258
19.10%	$87,977	($34,646)	$53,331	$460,612	$548,589	$548,589
0.03%	$176	($37,647)	($37,471)	$510,942	$511,118	$511,118
18.38%	$87,288	($36,095)	$51,193	$475,023	$562,311	$562,311
19.10%	$99,966	($38,928)	$61,038	$523,383	$623,349	$623,349
19.10%	$112,068	($36,608)	$75,460	$586,742	$698,809	$698,809
0.00%	$0	($40,547)	($40,547)	$658,262	$658,262	$658,262
19.10%	$118,340	($38,680)	$79,660	$619,582	$737,923	$737,923
0.00%	$0	($42,766)	($42,766)	$695,157	$695,157	$695,157
19.10%	$124,998	($40,715)	$84,283	$654,442	$779,440	**$779,440**
13.97%	$103,277	($40,260)	$63,017	$739,180	$842,457	$842,457
16.74%	$134,652	($37,869)	$96,783	$804,588	$939,240	$939,240
1.31%	$11,834	($35,594)	($23,760)	$903,646	$915,480	$915,480
14.80%	$131,234	($28,764)	$102,470	$886,716	$1,017,950	$1,017,950
13.70%	$136,128	($24,312)	$111,817	$993,638	$1,129,766	$1,129,766
13.70%	$151,355	($24,982)	$126,373	$1,104,784	$1,256,140	$1,256,140
10.08%	$123,974	($26,805)	$97,169	$1,229,334	$1,353,309	$1,353,309
13.70%	$181,421	($29,068)	$152,353	$1,324,241	$1,505,662	$1,505,662
13.70%	$201,830	($32,451)	$169,379	$1,473,211	$1,675,041	$1,675,041
0.00%	$0	($36,227)	($36,227)	$1,638,814	$1,638,814	**$1,638,814**
0.00%	$0	($35,995)	($35,995)	$1,602,819	$1,602,819	$1,602,819
13.70%	$214,674	($35,857)	$178,817	$1,566,962	$1,781,636	$1,781,636
13.70%	$238,596	($40,057)	$198,540	$1,741,579	$1,980,176	$1,980,176
13.70%	$265,155	($44,741)	$220,413	$1,935,435	$2,200,589	$2,200,589
11.93%	$256,653	($49,965)	$206,688	$2,150,624	$2,407,277	$2,407,277
13.70%	$322,247	($55,113)	$267,134	$2,352,165	$2,674,411	$2,674,411
0.00%	$0	($61,524)	($61,524)	$2,612,888	$2,612,888	$2,612,888
0.00%	$0	($61,588)	($61,588)	$2,551,300	$2,551,300	$2,551,300
10.90%	$271,403	($61,958)	$209,544	$2,489,442	$2,760,844	$2,760,844
0.00%	$0	($67,718)	($67,718)	$2,693,126	$2,693,126	**$2,693,126**
	$3,620,487	-$1,427,361	$2,193,126			

Credit (%) is depicted in column 10. Depending on the *Total Index Credit (%)* each year, the *Total Index Credits ($)* are determined by multiplying column 10 by the *End-Of-Year Value After Charges Before Credit* (column 14). You will notice that in years wherein the index credit was 0.00%, the *Total Index Credits ($)* column shows a $0 index credit (column 11). You will also notice that in some years, the values in the *Total Index Credits ($)* column (column 11) are greater than the *Total Charges ($)* in column 12, resulting in a *Year-End Gain* (column 13), and in other years, the charges were greater than the credits, resulting in a *Year-End Loss*.

These gains/losses are reflected in the *End-Of-Year Gross Index Account Value* (column 15). The total cumulative third-party lender debt (if any exist in that year) is then backed out of column 15, as is any internal carrier debt balance incurred by any *Participating Loans*, creating an *End-Of-Year Net Index Account Value* (column 16), which is a proxy for the *IUL's Cash Value*.

YEAR	AGE	1 INCOME DRAWDOWNS PARTICIPATING LOANS	2 CUMULATIVE ACCRUED INTERNAL LOAN PRINCIPAL	3 ACCRUED INTERNAL LOAN INTEREST	4 INDEX CREDIT AFTER CHARGES
1	50	$0	$0	$0	$0
2	51	$0	$0	$0	$0
3	52	$0	$0	$0	$0
4	53	$0	$0	$0	$0
5	54	$0	$0	$0	$0
6	55	$0	$0	$0	$0
7	56	$0	$0	$0	$0
8	57	$0	$0	$0	$0
9	58	$0	$0	$0	$0
10	59	$0	$0	$0	$0
11	60	$0	$0	$0	$0
12	61	$0	$0	$0	$0
13	62	$0	$0	$0	$0
14	63	$0	$0	$0	$0
15	64	$0	$0	$0	$0
16	65	-$58,742	-$58,742	-$2,643	$5,567
17	66	-$61,393	-$122,778	-$5,525	$0
18	67	-$52,588	-$180,892	-$8,140	$17,435
19	68	-$55,830	-$244,862	-$11,019	$0
20	69	-$46,804	-$302,684	-$13,621	$30,505
21	70	-$50,670	-$366,975	-$16,514	$31,970
22	71	-$51,985	-$435,474	-$19,596	$51,691
23	72	-$56,324	-$511,394	-$23,013	$5,529
24	73	-$48,097	-$582,504	-$26,213	$73,114
25	74	-$52,788	-$661,504	-$29,768	$89,637
26	75	-$57,691	-$748,962	-$33,703	$107,590
27	76	-$63,219	-$845,885	-$38,065	$94,602
28	77	-$64,954	-$948,903	-$42,701	$147,829
29	78	-$71,743	-$1,063,347	-$47,851	$175,100
30	79	-$79,317	-$1,190,514	-$53,573	$0
31	80	-$65,196	-$1,309,283	-$58,918	$0
32	81	-$51,820	-$1,420,022	-$63,901	$218,211
33	82	-$60,776	-$1,544,699	-$69,511	$254,023
34	83	-$70,599	-$1,684,809	-$75,816	$295,696
35	84	-$81,386	-$1,842,011	-$82,891	$299,762
36	85	-$89,405	-$2,014,307	-$90,644	$393,872
37	86	-$102,337	-$2,207,287	-$99,328	$0
38	87	-$80,287	-$2,386,903	-$107,411	$0
39	88	-$59,369	-$2,553,682	-$114,916	$374,801
40	89	-$67,109	-$2,735,707	-$123,107	$0
		-$1,600,428		-$1,258,386	$2,666,935

The above ledger is different than the one on the previous pages. This one depicts the correlation between the *Participating Loan* debt and the *Index Credits* received in the *Index Account* when drawing down tax-free retirement income from the policy value using a *Participating Loan*. Personally, I think it is important to transparently show clients examples wherein their net account value may decrease in a given year due to the internal interest charged on *Participating Loans*, despite the 0.00% floor.

This ledger above shows the tax-free retirement income drawdowns (column 1) during the 40-year period that produced the *Worst Compounded Annual Growth Rate* out of 121 different 40-year periods analyzed. The interest charged using a *Participating Loan Rate (PLR)* of 4.50% is accrued (column 3) and rolled into the *Cumulative Accrued Internal Loan Principal* (column 2).

5 CUMULATIVE INTERNAL DEBT BALANCE	6 CUMULATIVE INDEXED LOAN ACCOUNT VALUE	7 CUMULATIVE PAR LOAN GAIN/LOSS	8 EOY GROSS INDEX ACCUMULATED VALUE	9 EOY INDEX VALUE NET OF INT & EXT LOANS
$0	$0	$0	$45,320	$31,040
$0	$0	$0	$85,542	$72,847
$0	$0	$0	$124,617	$113,508
$0	$0	$0	$185,845	$176,327
$0	$0	$0	$255,160	$247,228
$0	$0	$0	$286,914	$280,566
$0	$0	$0	$349,941	$345,185
$0	$0	$0	$419,783	$416,613
$0	$0	$0	$523,238	$521,653
$0	$0	$0	$535,258	**$535,258**
$0	$0	$0	$542,485	$542,485
$0	$0	$0	$612,110	$612,110
$0	$0	$0	$580,239	$580,239
$0	$0	$0	$650,679	$650,679
$0	$0	$0	$734,275	$734,275
-$61,385	$69,962	**$8,576**	$828,798	$767,412
-$128,303	$131,355	**$3,051**	$785,659	$657,356
-$189,032	$219,076	**$30,044**	$886,903	$697,871
-$255,880	$274,906	**$19,026**	$840,930	$585,050
-$316,305	$383,157	**$66,851**	$949,677	**$633,372**
-$383,489	$494,440	**$110,951**	$1,033,302	$649,813
-$455,070	$637,872	**$182,802**	$1,159,120	$704,049
-$534,407	$703,288	**$168,881**	$1,135,619	$601,212
-$608,717	$862,589	**$253,873**	$1,268,561	$659,844
-$691,272	$1,040,784	**$349,512**	$1,412,403	$721,132
-$782,666	$1,248,965	**$466,299**	$1,572,901	$790,236
-$883,949	$1,444,513	**$560,564**	$1,695,876	$811,926
-$991,604	$1,716,265	**$724,660**	$1,888,386	$896,782
-$1,111,197	$2,032,964	**$921,767**	$2,102,656	$991,459
-$1,244,087	$2,112,281	**$868,194**	$2,059,042	**$814,955**
-$1,368,201	$2,177,477	**$809,276**	$2,015,957	$647,756
-$1,483,923	$2,534,711	**$1,050,789**	$2,243,624	$759,702
-$1,614,210	$2,951,069	**$1,336,859**	$2,496,694	$882,484
-$1,760,625	$3,435,637	**$1,675,011**	$2,777,948	$1,017,322
-$1,924,902	$3,936,739	**$2,011,838**	$3,042,463	$1,117,562
-$2,104,950	$4,577,726	**$2,472,776**	$3,384,164	$1,279,214
-$2,306,615	$4,680,063	**$2,373,448**	$3,310,204	$1,003,589
-$2,494,313	$4,760,350	**$2,266,037**	$3,236,421	$742,108
-$2,668,597	$5,345,172	**$2,676,574**	$3,507,462	$838,864
-$2,858,813	$5,412,281	**$2,553,468**	$3,426,681	**$567,868**

The income drawdowns (column 1) are credited using the same S&P 500-correlated floor/cap index crediting method, receiving a positive index credit during years when the S&P 500 generates a positive return, and credits $0 during years wherein the S&P 500 produces a negative return (column 4).

The *Cumulative Internal Debt Balance* from taking these *Participating Loans* (and being charged a *Participating Loan Rate* of 4.50%)is depicted in column 5, and the *Cumulative Index Balance On Participating Loans* is depicted in column 6, producing the *Cumulative Loan Gains/Losses* in column 7.

Due to using *Participating Loans* to generate the tax-free income drawdowns in years 16-40, the cumulative internal debt totals a negative $2,858,813 by year 40 (bottom of column 5).

However, the cumulative gains in the separate index account total $5,412,281 (bottom of column 6), resulting in a net gain of $2,553,468 in year 40 (bottom of column 7) due to the *Participating Loan* arrangement during the 40-Year period with the *Worst Compounded Annual Growth Rate* out of 121 different 40-year periods analyzed.

Every client should see this type of backtested scenario when considering an *IUL* as an estate planning strategy.

Without this backtesting analyzation, how would any know if this proposition would stand up during times of volatility?

Being able to show a client this type of modeling is invaluable because it shows that a tremendous effort was made in the areas of:

1. Full Transparency.
2. Client Education.
3. Consumer Protection.
4. Explaining How Volatility Can Produce a Range of Different Potential Outcomes.
5. Explaining The Relationship Between Credits and Charges.

Chapter 8
Volatility Controlled Indices

Several years ago, I was sitting in a conference room listening to a representative from a major wire house talking about something called a *Volatility Controlled Index (VCI)*. I was curious what this *non-S&P 500* index option was all about.

The representative talked about how their money managers could track market trends daily, and their ability to move money from equities to bonds (or bonds to equities) when their proprietary algorithm was triggered by market volatility. Their rationale behind this proposition (in addition to their self-proclaimed *crystal ball reading* ability) was that their actively managed index would reduce volatility, thus minimizing risk.

The concept had some merit on the surface. Similar to *Dollar Cost Averaging* and the diversifying of a managed portfolio, *VCIs* smooth out the ups and downs and in theory, limits the number of 0.00% returns an index could have (assuming a 0.00% floor). The theoretical trade off is that you would reduce your 0.00% crediting years in exchange for giving up some of your upside.

The reason I say the trade off is only *theoretical* is that an index with a 0.00% is already protecting your downside in exchange for a limitation in the maximum allowable return credited in a given year (the cap). This *Floor & Cap* proposition already manages volatility. To then manage the volatility within an already volatility-managed construct never made any sense to me.

In a *Floor & Cap* proposition with an IUL, volatility is actually your friend. Historically speaking, the *S&P 500* – during 40-year period between 1984-2023 – produced thirty positive returning years (75.00%). Of those thirty positive returning years, twenty-six were greater than 8.00% and twenty-one were greater than 10.00%.

There were only four years (out of those thirty positive returning years) that produced a return less than 8.00%. My point is that hitting the cap during the large majority of positive returning years offsets the 0.00% return years and potentially creates a nice positive arbitrage.

In a *VCI*, you just don't have the upside potential during positive returning years the way you do in an *S&P 500* index due to the lack of equities in the index – again, in *theory*.

Now, does this mean *VCIs* are bad?

Not at all.

VCIs are however under major scrutiny and criticism at the moment – some of which is warranted, and some not so much. One of the criticisms of *VCIs* is that they have been illustrating crediting assumptions based on multi-decade historical returns, despite the fact that some of these index options had only been created a few short years ago. The rationale behind them using this backtested historical data was that it was possible to take the same index components (the actual equities and non-equities in the current *VCI*) and rebuild a clone of the *VCI*, tracking what the historical performance would have been had the *VCI* actually existed back then.

But that is like a professional baseball team saying their scouting and player development program is superior because it *would have* picked Barry Bonds, Mark McGwire, Tony Gwynn, and Ken Griffey, Jr. in the 1980's before they knew what kind of players they would develop into in the 1990's. Knowing what we know now about these players, of course they would have drafted them back when they entered the draft. Conversely, there have been several big-time prospects that many thought would become big league superstars, yet never reached their projected potential – players like Chipper Jones and Billy Beane.

If we look at the historical returns of just a few *VCIs* compared to *S&P 500* index returns using a floor and cap crediting method, it is very easy to take pieces of such data and draw assumptions that may or may not hold water over time. It is also easy to manipulate statistics to fit a particular narrative, and though the statistics themselves may be true, the assumptions that are drawn out of these statistics may lead someone to believe something that is out of context.

As an example, it is a historically statistical proven fact that 100% of all human babies that drink cow milk die. This is an indisputable proven fact, and will remain true for the rest of human life on this earth.

For the *dummies* reading this that don't understand what I just stated (and for those that lack a sense of humor), all babies that drink cow milk will die... eventually, even if it is at age 100. There's no correlation between drinking cow milk and the certain death that all mortal human beings will face eventually, however the statistical statement – which is indisputably true and mathematically correct – can be misconstrued to fit the narrative that there is something deadly about ingesting milk from a cow.

Let's take a moment to analyze some statistical, historically accurate data in regards to comparing the historical performance of a few *VCIs* with different *Participation Rates* (which varied from year to year) to the historical performance of an *S&P 500-Correlated* index with a 0.00% floor, a cap (which varied from year to year), and a 0.50% bonus.

NATIONAL LIFE GROUP
CREDIT SUISSE
YEAR INDEX STARTED: 2017
2024 PAR RATE: 215%

CALENDAR YEAR	VCI RETURN		PAR RATE		INDEX CREDIT
2019	10.40%	x	130.00%	=	13.52%
2020	4.10%	x	130.00%	=	5.33%
2021	8.90%	x	130.00%	=	11.57%
2022	-2.30%	x	130.00%	=	0.00%
2023	2.80%	x	140.00%	=	3.92%
AVERAGE	**4.78%**		**132.00%**		**6.87%**

*Sourced directly from https://indices.credit-suisse.com/CSTRENDS

ALLIANZ
PIMCO TACTICAL BALANCED ER
YEAR INDEX STARTED: 2018
2024 PAR RATE: 185%

CALENDAR YEAR	VCI RETURN		PAR RATE		INDEX CREDIT
2019	10.35%	x	155.00%	=	16.04%
2020	4.07%	x	155.00%	=	6.31%
2021	8.94%	x	140.00%	=	12.52%
2022	-2.27%	x	160.00%	=	0.00%
2023	2.79%	x	175.00%	=	4.88%
AVERAGE	**4.78%**		**157.00%**		**7.95%**

*Sourced directly from Allianz CSI-517 (R-22024)

NATIONWIDE
JP MORGAN MOSAIC II
YEAR INDEX STARTED: 2016
2024 PAR RATE: 190%

CALENDAR YEAR	VCI RETURN		PAR RATE		INDEX CREDIT
2019	7.15%	x	125.00%	=	8.94%
2020	-1.69%	x	135.00%	=	0.00%
2021	6.11%	x	135.00%	=	8.25%
2022	-9.56%	x	140.00%	=	0.00%
2023	1.29%	x	195.00%	=	2.52%
AVERAGE	**0.66%**		**146.00%**		**3.94%**

*Sourced directly from Nationwide via email on 4/23/2024

PENN MUTUAL
S&P 500 PT-TO-PT
YEAR INDEX STARTED: 1957
2024 CAP: 10.25%

CALENDAR YEAR	S&P 500 RETURN		INDEX CAP		INDEX CREDIT
2019	31.74%	=	10.50%	=	10.50%
2020	18.38%	=	10.00%	=	10.00%
2021	28.83%	=	9.50%	=	9.50%
2022	-19.44%	=	9.50%	=	0.00%
2023	24.23%	=	10.25%	=	10.75%**
AVERAGE	**16.75%**		**9.95%**		**8.15%**

*Sourced directly from Penn Mutual   **Index Credit Assumes a 50bp bonus

The *Pro-VCI Advocates* will look at these numbers and gloat that the average returns of two of the three *VCIs* over the last five years have out-produced the *S&P 500* index with the floor and cap, however that is only (and conveniently) only a 5-year period where their proposition proofed positive (similar to the baseball draft analogy I used earlier). But any reasonable person could easily argue that a 5-year period is far too short a window of time to draw any long-term assumptions from.

The *Anti-VCI Critics* will gloat that in 2023, the *S&P 500* index with the floor and cap would have produced a 10.75% return, whereas the best producing *VCI* in that year only produced a 6.08% return. Their assumption might be that in today's environment, *VCIs* are not appropriate. During high interest rate environments (similar to today's interest rate environment), *VCIs* typically do as well as *S&P 500* index funds with a floor and cap, however that does not mean that *VCIs* are bad.

But this *Anti-VCI Critics'* gloating is based on *Monday Morning Quarterback* intel. As a parallel example, building a portfolio that took heavy positions in of *Blockbuster Video* and *Circuit City* in the late 1990's would have seemed pretty smart in the early 2000's because of their historical success. However *Circuit City* filed bankruptcy in 2008, and *Blockbuster Video* closed their last store in the United States in 2019. It would be easy for a *so-called stock market expert* to say, *"Nobody should have invested in these companies"* after the fact, but that is a fool's gloat.

It is easy to play *Monday Morning Quarterback*.

Now, there is – in theory – an advantage to having an uncapped upside the way many *VCIs* do. The concept of an uncapped upside means there is no limit to the gains you could make, however the fact that it is volatility-controlled means the equities allocation within the *VCI* is not as heavy as non-equities (like bonds).

As an example, in 2023, these are the equities-to-non-equities allocations of the three different *VCIs* I just mentioned.

VOLATILITY CONTROLLED INDEX	EQUITIES	NON-EQUITIES
JP MORGAN MOSAIC II	29.00%	71.00%
PIMCO TACTICAL BALANCED ER	23.00%	77.00%
CREDIT SUISSE	25.00%	75.00%

As you can see, when the equities position is less than 30.00% within an indexed fund, the upside is going to be limited due to heavy diversification into non-equities.

However, to offset the lower returns that typically come with heavy allocations in non-equities funds (like bonds for example), these aforementioned *VCIs* have *Participation Bonuses* that range from 190.00% to 215.00%. In other words, if the *VCI* produced a gross return of 4.00%, assuming a 200.00% participation rate, the actual return in that year would be 8.00% (4.00% x 200% = 8.00%). Most of these *VCIs* also have a 0.00% floor and an uncapped upside, so the 0.00% floor protects the downside... the uncapped upside doesn't limit the upside potential (the way a capped index would), and the volatility-controlled component further mitigates risk, in theory.

The proposition here is, *"The VCI only needs to produce a 4.00% in order to get 8.00%. 4.00% is nothing."*

This proposition – though easy to explain – is not as simple in its construction. As you saw in the historical comparison between *VCI* performance versus *S&P 500* performance, there are several moving parts, and just because one may have worked better in select instances does not mean that one is necessarily universally better in all scenarios.

Perhaps you are wondering how these *Participation Bonus* rates are determined. In order for the index fund to offer a *Participation Bonus*, there is something called the *Risk-Free Rate*. Think of it as the *cost* or spread deducted from the gross *VCI* return.

When *VCIs* first gained popularity, the *Risk-Free Rate* was 0.00%, however today's *Risk-Free Rates* hover around 5.30% (similar to the *SOFR* rate or the *FedFunds* rate). As an example, if the *VCI* with a 200.00% *Participation Rate* produced a 9.30% gross return, after the *Risk-Free Rate* cost deduction, the *pre-Participation Bonus* return would be 4.00% (9.30% - 5.30% = 4.00%). If the *Participating Rate* was 200.00%, the *VCI* index credit in such year would be 8.00% (4.00% x 200.00% = 8.00%).

As I said, that easy-to-explain articulation of *Participation Bonus* rates is not as simple as only needing a 4.00% return to get

8.00%. Back when the *Risk-Free Rate* was 0.00%, this simple statement was true. In today's environment, it is not so simple.

So why was there such a heavy push in the industry advocating *VCIs* a few years ago? I have my theory. This is purely speculative, however I think my logic is sound.

Due to *AG-49A*, the regulators had their way with emasculating *IUL* illustrations, as I discussed earlier in this book. But what the regulators missed was the ability for a carrier to illustrated certain bonus assumptions in a *VCI* that was forbidden in an *S&P 500* point-to-point illustration. This loophole allowed carriers to illustrate more favorable outcomes in a *VCI* illustration.

One of the things that has always driven me crazy in the life insurance industry is the fact that most advisors *sell* the client solely based on the numbers and outcomes depicted in the carrier illustration. Since most insurance agents are actually brokers – meaning they can sell virtually any insurance carrier they so choose – they will typically sell the carrier that shows the best outcomes in their illustration. This is such a poor method for a client to choose the carrier and *IUL* that is right for them.

As I mentioned in the chapter about backtesting, understanding the relationship between charges and the crediting methodology only truly becomes apparent when we backtest these assumptions during times of volatility. Just because one product performs better when using positive static return assumptions every year (the way a carrier illustration depicts outcomes) does not mean that same product will perform better than other alternatives during times of volatility.

Since there is not enough historical data with any of these new *VCIs*, I cannot provide a true backtesting report with a *VCI*. Again, this doesn't mean that *VCIs* are bad.

The reality is, you need to make a philosophical decision regarding diversification and risk mitigation when it comes to choosing either a *VCI* or an *S&P 500* index allocation. I have had some clients elect a *VCI* a couple of years ago because interest rates were low and the client speculated that the stock market would not produce a very good return. They guessed wrong. Interest rates skyrocketed over the last couple of years and though the *S&P 500* produced a negative return in 2023 (-19.44%), in 2023, it produced a positive 24.33% return.

Their decision to opt for a *VCI* was not philosophically incorrect. They made the best decision they could at that time, and though they guessed wrong, it is not the end of the world. They have the ability to switch to an *S&P 500-correlated index* at their next policy renewal.

In summary regarding *VCIs*, it is foolish to say that they are better than *S&P 500* index options, and vice-versa. Personally, I still stand by the philosophy I have had since the inception of *VCIs* (as well as *Dollar Cost Averaging*) – that there is nothing wrong with either of these strategies – however regarding *IULs,* I am philosophically opposed to both. Always remember that in an *IUL* with a floor and cap, volatility is your friend.

Chapter 9
My Own IUL

I own a fairly large *IUL* policy on my life, and my wife owns an *IUL* on her life as well. In this short chapter, I'll briefly explain why we chose to invest in these assets, and perhaps you will glean some perspective on the value of using an *IUL* in this capacity.

We chose this asset class for several reasons. Though I'm not a billionaire, I have a relatively high income, and being in the top income tax bracket living in California (currently 37.00% Federal Income Tax + 3.80% Medicare Tax + $13.30% California State Income Tax = **54.10%**), I love the idea of parking money in a tax-free asset that accumulates with a stop-loss feature (the 0% floor in my *IUL* policy).

When I assess whether or not an *IUL* is suitable for a specific client, I break down their adult life into three different stages:

    I. Income-Earning Years.
    II. Retirement Years.
    III. Twilight Years.

I'll use my own situation as a real world example.

During *Stage I* of my adult life – *My Income-Earning Years* – I have a substantial personal overhead with a $2.1 million mortgage on my primary residence, another mortgage on my vacation home in Hawaii, private school tuition for my son, lifestyle expenses, etc. My family relies on my earned income to facilitate our lifestyle.

I need to insure the loss of my earned income in the event that I die unexpectedly early. It may sound morbid to think about, but if I fall victim to a fatal car accident tomorrow, or if I die of cancer during my income-earning years, or if my life is ended by some other common tragedy, my family would not be able to maintain their lifestyle and pay our current living expenses without my earned income.

The purpose of my policy's death benefit is to provide my family with the liquidity they need to keep our family home and maintain the comfortable lifestyle they enjoy now. I don't *plan* on dying early, but I've never met a cancer victim who *planned* to die early either.

Now, if I am blessed enough to live a nice long healthy life, I will enter *Stage II* of my adult life – *My Retirement Years*. By that time, my mortgage will likely be paid off, my son will be a financially independent adult, and my overhead expenses may be lower than they are today. At that point, perhaps I will not need as much death benefit as I need today, so I have the option of drawing down a tax-free retirement income stream from my policy.

All the while during *My Income-Earning Years*, the cash value is accumulating tax-free, and is also protected from market crashes due to the 0.00% floor. These tax advantages and downside protection are extremely appealing to me, and I have found that many clients, CPAs, and estate planning attorneys share a similar perspective on these matters.

I don't know anyone that thinks income tax rates are going to go down. Given this belief, the tax-free growth and tax-free income drawdowns from an *IUL* policy are of tremendous value. From a tax standpoint, it is kind of like a *Roth-IRA-For-The-Wealthy* that also has a 0.00% floor AND a death benefit.

That's one heck of a powerful combination.

One of my websites – **Rothish.com** – explains this concept in an easy-to-follow video. It's not a *Roth IRA*, but it's taxed like a *Roth*, so it's kind of *Rothish*.

Then if I'm extremely blessed, I will one day enter *Stage III* of my adult life – *My Twilight Years*. If things go moderately well, even after I take substantial tax-free income drawdowns from my policy, there will still be a death benefit that I will leave behind for my son (and my future grandkids, if I'm so lucky to have them one day).

In my both my wife's *IUL* and my *IUL* – due to my net worth and income – we chose to use a *partially premium financed* design wherein we paid the first year premium out-of-pocket for each policy. Then starting in year two, we used a bank to finance the remaining multi-six figure premiums, and we pay the interest due on the cumulative loan balance each year. This is a strategy that high net worth clients often use (I alluded to this concept of *Premium Financing* earlier in this book).

If a client is considering paying an annual premium of $100,000 per year (or greater), they might want to consider using one of my five *Premium Financing* methods.

For my wife's policy, we evaluated paying a non-financed premium out-of-pocket each year versus paying about the same cumulative amount in the form of *Premium Financing Loan Interest*. We found that using leverage – in her specific situation – produced more than double the death benefit compared to a non-financed policy, and more than double the tax-free retirement income drawdowns compared to the non-financed design using the exact same *IUL* product.

There are obviously financial underwriting requirements in order to use *Premium Financing*. Below are just a few insurance carrier net worth minimum requirements, from highest to lowest:

Penn Mutual: $15MM
Pacific Life: $10MM
Nationwide: $10MM
Transamerica: $5MM
Securian: $5MM
National Life Group (LSW): $2.5MM
Lincoln: $2.5MM (ages 30-50), $5MM (ages 51+)
Allianz: $1MM, or $500K NW with $200K income, or $0 NW with $400K income

If you are interested in learning more about how *Premium Financing* works, I recommend reading one of my books called **Premium Financed Life Insurance – The Key To Effective Estate Tax Planning**.

But even if your net worth is nowhere close to these numbers above, and you are thinking of contributing less than $100,000 per year in premium, an *IUL* might still be a great retirement planning instrument for you.

I have seen some people contribute as little as $200 per month towards an *IUL*. Of course this doesn't buy millions of dollars of life insurance, but if you are considering contributing towards some sort of retirement plan (even a modest amount), and you like the idea of tax-free gains, the downside protection of a 0% floor, and you would like to have some life insurance to protect your family if you were to die unexpectedly early, an *IUL* might be a great solution for your situation.

In fact, I put a non-financed *IUL* on my son when he was only 4-years old. We only contribute $300 per month towards his *IUL*. His cash value will grow tax-free, he has the protection of the 0% floor, and one day we will transfer the ownership of this policy from us to him. He will undoubtedly be glad we put this in place for him at such a young age, both from a *Cash Value Accumulation* standpoint AND a *Death Benefit* standpoint.

In addition, I have some clients that are not even close to being as wealthy as my *Premium Financing* clients, and they contribute $500 to $1,000 a month towards their *IULs*.

I share these other client examples with you because though the *IUL* product was originally designed for multi-six-figure and seven-figure income earners, it can be an extremely efficient retirement income planning tool for those with far lower incomes.

So in summary, is an *IUL* right for you?

Conceptually, an *IUL* might be a great option for you if:

1. You want to protect your family with life insurance in case you die unexpectedly early during your *Income-Earning Years*.
2. You like the idea of generating a tax-free retirement income during your *Retirement Years*.
3. You like the idea of a 0% floor to protect you from market crashes.

Even if you don't care about protecting your family with life insurance, the tax-free income and 0% floor are two incredibly valuable attributes.

For me and my family, the *IUL* gives me piece of mind that if I die unexpectedly early, my family is protected… and if I don't, I'll have a nice tax-free retirement income stream waiting for me.

Chapter 10
History Of The Author

So why should you listen to me?

A wise man once said, *"If you don't know the history of the author, then you don't know what you're reading."*

That being said, I will share with you my background, how I got into this highly specialized line of work, as well as the current scope of my business.

When most people hear that I finance $50 million to $100 million life insurance policies for uber-wealthy clients, they often think I grew up around extremely wealthy people. Perhaps they think I spend my time at private country clubs sipping on overpriced cocktails holding my martini glass with my little pinky finger up in the air, hobnobbing with the likes of *Thurston Howell, III*.

Nothing could be further from the truth. I started my career in the insurance industry in 2003 after I decided to end my career as high school teacher in Hawaii. I moved back to Long Beach, California where I was born and raised and entered the insurance industry at age thirty-one. I got my start in the employee benefits arena, selling health insurance programs to small companies, and let me tell you, it was not as easy as I thought it was going to be.

The *California State Department of Insurance* issued my insurance license on January 3, 2003, and to say that 2003 was a *rough year* would be the understatement of a lifetime. I first solicited people I knew – my friends and family – and tried to get them to buy insurance from me. To my chagrin, most of them declined my offers. So I started cold calling businesses, and as you can probably imagine, my results were even more dismal. Nobody wanted to talk to me, and perhaps I couldn't blame them, for I was a brand new insurance agent with no experience.

My 2003 personal tax return showed a total income of $277 for the entire year. I actually have a copy of it framed on the wall of my office.

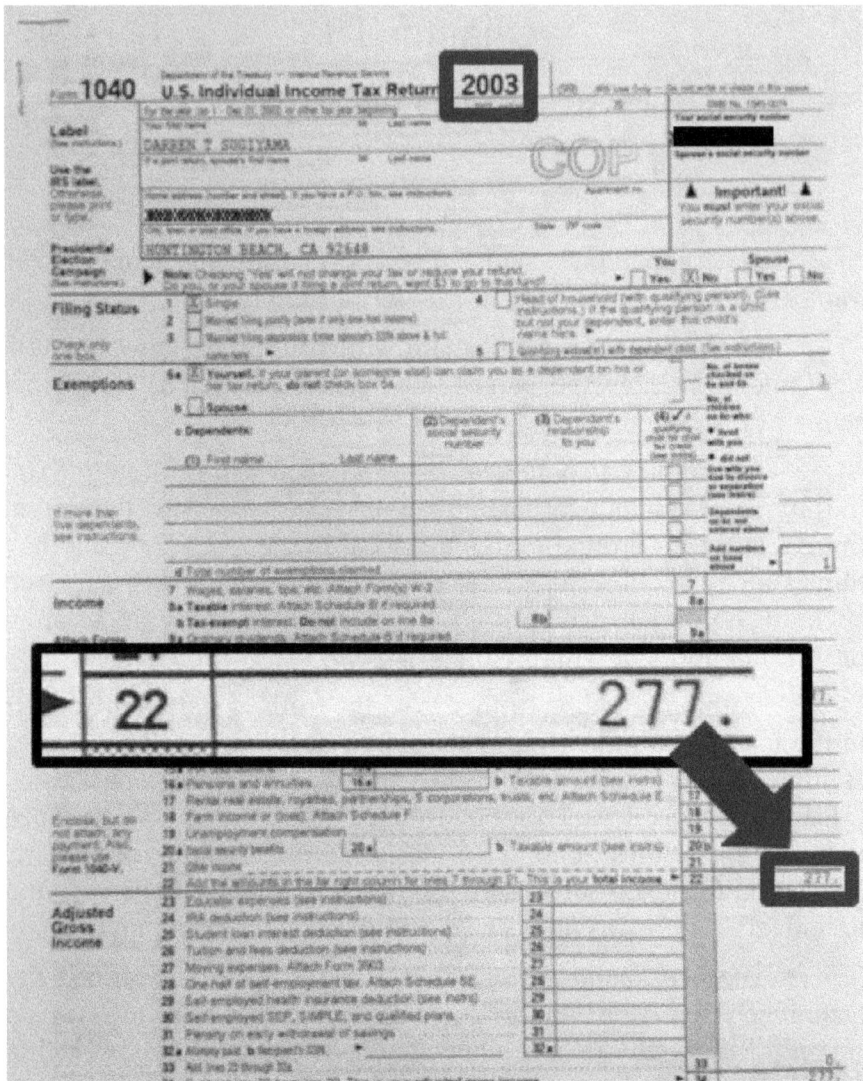

Darren Sugiyama's 2003 Personal Tax Return showing an income of $277 for the year.

I think it's important for all of us to remember where we came from. It keeps us humble and grounded, regardless of how much success we may have achieved in our lives. Looking at my 2003 tax return on my wall every day is a great reminder that I didn't always have the caliber of clientele I have today.

After spending my first year in the insurance industry trying to emulate what other successful insurance agents have done (and failing miserably at it), I decided to do something extremely unconventional.

I took a step back – taking an outsider's view of the industry – and started designing an entirely different client proposition. I took a strategy that large corporations were using in their employee benefit packages, scaled it down, and re-engineered it into a new platform for small businesses that didn't have access to big company benefits.

Everyone in the insurance industry told me that my vision of reinventing the wheel was a bad idea, but after two years of recalibrating my platform based on what I *thought* small company employee benefits *could* be, my unconventional methodology began to get traction. I took my idea to two different *TPAs (Third-Party Administrators)* and built a white-labeled semi-self-funded strategy using supplemental insurance products from specialty carriers in conjunction with the major medical carriers.

Five years into my insurance career, I had built one of the fastest growing employee benefits firms in the industry. My firm, *Apex Outsourcing* was the #1 producing firm in the country for *Kaiser Permanente, HealthNet,* and *Colonial Life* concurrently; the #2 firm in the State of California for *Aetna*; top 30 in California for *Blue Cross*; and by my seventh year in the business, my firm had topped over $37 million in annual recurring premium.

I actually wrote a book about it called **How I Built A $37 Million Insurance Agency In Less Than 7 Years**, and it has become one of the insurance industry's most notorious books ever published. In fact, if you search the term *Insurance Agency* on *Amazon*, the first edition of my book pops up on the first page and has more reviews than any other book in its category. I have since written a *Second Edition* version of this book as well.

When I originally wrote that book, I was in my mid 30's and I met a so-called financial advisor that implemented a very elaborate life insurance-based financial strategy within my company. To make a very long story short, his recommendations ended up losing me $930,000 within a three-year period of time.

This experience absolutely enraged me, but as angry as I was, I was far more embarrassed. I thought I was a reasonably smart person, but taking that kind of financial loss made me feel naïve. It made me feel violated. It made me feel stupid.

I spent the next year obsessively studying every life insurance product in the market, learning about how each product chassis was built, how the crediting methods work, how the underlying investments work, and how the policy charges work. I took those lemons I was dealt and decided to make a lemonade factory.

I ended up writing another book called ***Ouch: How My Financial Advisor Lost Me $930,000 In Three Years***. The concepts I wrote about in that book served as the foundation of building my second insurance agency – *DaVinci Financial* – this time specializing in life insurance for business owners. We used that book to teach our clients how to avoid what happened to me.

I built *DaVinci* into a sizable firm in Orange County, California that at one point housed over forty life insurance agents and financial advisors, plus I also built additional satellite offices in Las Vegas, Nevada; Hartford, Connecticut; Seattle, Washington; Dallas, Texas; and Manhattan, New York. Eventually, we became responsible for over 24% of all the life insurance policies sold in Orange County, California for *Pacific Life* in 2017, over 29% for *Penn Mutual* in 2018, and over 38% for *Penn Mutual* in 2019. Almost all of these life insurance policies we sold at that time were relatively small *IULs* (our average client monthly premium was only $203). These clients were working class Americans – employees of companies owned by wealth business owners.

I was running both *Apex* and *DaVinci* concurrently, and in 2016, I started building *Lionsmark Capital*, my premium financing intermediary firm. *Lionsmark* quickly became known as the most mathematically-sound premium financing intermediary in the insurance industry.

Entering the niche space of premium financing back in 2016 – especially as an intermediary – was a counter-intuitive thing for me to do by most people's standards. I already had two successful multi-agent insurance agencies – one employee benefits firm and one life insurance firm – and so doubling down on building a premium financing intermediary firm was a big decision for me. But I identified two glaring deficiencies in the premium financing industry – two vitally important things that every client and advisor was silently begging for: *Transparency* and *Client Education*.

I felt it was time for me to innovate again – to reinvent another *new wheel*. Most people thought I was crazy for making this shift, but similar to my two previous insurance ventures, I was confident that my unorthodox approach and fresh perspective could disrupt the entire industry. I didn't want to merely build a *better* version of a premium financing intermediary firm. I wanted to create an entirely different client experience, as well as give advisors a completely new intermediary experience. As I said, I wanted to reinvent a *new wheel*.

Back in 2013, I started building an algorithmically-based software solution that could backtest and stress-test *Indexed Universal Life (IUL)* insurance policies' crediting methods. I started out by using these backtesting models in *DaVinci*, but I wanted to be able to expand my software solution into modeling premium financing arrangements, especially during times of volatility. No one in the life insurance industry was doing anything like this, and even to this day, no one has been able to replicate it.

I went to all the *advanced markets* attorneys at the major insurance carriers and explained what I was doing because I wanted to make sure I wasn't violating any compliance regulations. I emphatically clarified that my models were not recreations of *insurance policy illustrations*, rather they were hypothetical synthetic models that would help educate clients on how different elements of these products actually work; things like floors, caps, charges, and multiplier bonuses.

The spirit of my work has always been rooted in *client education* – probably a subconscious effort to continue my teaching career in a reimagined way.

When I first started implementing these mathematically-based models in premium financing back in 2017, *Lionsmark* primarily used a direct-to-consumer business model whose clientele was mostly small business owners. I felt that this was a great way for me to launch *Lionsmark* because I could control 100% of the point-of-sale process, refining our reimagined way of positioning premium financing. I had two in-house marketing agents that cold called business owners in thirty different states.

We used a virtual point-of-sale business model, selling over the phone, long before *COVID-19* and *Zoom*, back when people told me that *no one* would buy *Premium Financed Life Insurance* over the phone, never having met us. The reality is, people told me the same thing about employee benefits, yet *Apex* sold group health insurance over the phone and email, and *DaVinci* sold life insurance using a virtual model as well. With *Lionsmark*, we used the same business model of *virtual selling* I perfected back in 2009 using an auto-dialer I custom built in-house. My system dialed 400 dials per day per agent.

I still remember the first premium financing case we wrote. A client in Nebraska opted for our platform we used to call *Leveraged Index Arbitrage*, wherein the client paid the first year premium out-of-pocket, and financing started in either year two or year three. This client sent us a first-year premium check for $400,000 – to a firm he's never heard of – to an agent he's never met that cold called him out of the blue. At that point, I realized my unconventional model of doing business *virtually* in an industry that was used to doing things face-to-face would work once again, even with the high net worth market. Of course we all do *Zoom* meetings now, but back in 2017, this was unheard of.

Once word started getting out that we had a superior technology-based backtesting and stress-testing method – as well as a proprietary way to mitigate client risk – other advisors began to inquire. My *ex-competitors* became my *referral sources,* and I am now one of their most trusted resources when it comes to interfacing with their most valuable clients.

By 2018, my reputation in the industry began to evolve from being *a guy that builds large insurance agencies*, to *THE guy that does premium financing the RIGHT way.*

I started receiving requests to speak at industry events as a premium financing expert. The first major speaking engagement happened on November 7, 2018 where I was asked to speak at

Simplicity Life's Premium Financing Symposium in Houston, Texas.

I still remember hearing the *Senior Vice-President of Premium Financing* from a large bank explain that they only lend annual premiums of $1,000,000 or greater, which resulted in a total loan facility of $7,000,000 to $10,000,000.

I remember thinking to myself, *"Whoa, those are some big policies."* Back then, our average-sized policies were about a third of that. Fast forward to my current client demographic, a $1,000,000 annual premium with a $10,000,000 loan facility has become my *new normal*.

On March 19, 2019, I spoke from stage at *FFR's Spring Symposium* at *The Montage Resort* in Laguna Beach, California on how I approach premium financing in a completely different and reimagined way.

Darren Sugiyama speaking at FFR's 2019 Spring Symposium.

That *FFR* speaking engagement was a major pivotal moment for me because of the exposure it gave me to a larger audience: Advisors, Carrier Executives, Wholesalers, and Distribution Partners. It really cemented my reputation as being an expert in the premium financing arena, sending a message to the entire industry that I was now a force to be reckoned with.

Later that month, I was invited to speak at *Penn Mutual's Advance Planning Council* in Irvine, California as the subject expert on premium financing, and the very next month in April, I spoke at another event at their regional office in Chicago, Illinois.

Later that year in August 2019, *Nationwide* hosted a premium financing symposium at their corporate office in Columbus, Ohio, and *Lionsmark Capital* was the only *non-Nationwide* presenter at their entire symposium. In that same year, I wrote a book called *The Definitive Book On Premium Financing* that quickly became, well, the definitive book on premium financing.

In the midst of the 2020 pandemic, *Pacific Life* held their *National Symposium* virtually, and I was a featured speaker as the subject expert on *IUL* multipliers. I was chosen to speak about the charges and crediting methodologies used in their *PDX2* and *PIA6 IULs* alongside Stephan Mitchell – the *Assistant Vice President of Product Marketing at Pacific Life* at that time – who is someone that I have always had an immense amount of respect for as an *IUL* expert and product technician. I believe *Pacific Life's* decision to select me as a speaker for this nationally broadcasted event was largely due to the sophistication of my backtesting modeling capabilities.

I have been the featured speaker on premium financing at seminar and webinar events sponsored by other carriers including *John Hancock* and *Ohio National*, as well as other BGAs and producer groups like *AEG, Alpine Brokerage, BGA Insurance, Center for Tax Strategies & Resources, CPS, Elite Resource Team, The Producers Group, Redwood Tax Specialists,* and *Peloton* (an *IMO* that supports over 20 different *BGAs*).

This year in 2024, I was elected by *FFR's* 228 members to be one of their seven board members.

I know the previous few pages in this chapter probably sounded rather braggadocious, however I felt it was important to establish my background and credibility on this topic. As I said at the beginning of this book, a wise man once said, *"If you don't know* the history of the author, then you don't know what you're reading."

As my reputation in the life insurance industry grew, I began receiving strong endorsements from insurance carriers, investment broker-dealers, *IMOs*, and *BGAs*, publicly saying that *Lionsmark Capital* should be a financial advisor's *Hired Gun Of Choice* when it came to premium financing. This level of endorsement gave me the credibility I needed to grow my firm exponentially.

The financial professionals that I do business with today come from a variety of different disciplines, including financial advisors, CPAs, estate planning attorneys, family offices, and of course, life insurance agents. These professionals rely on me to not only secure the lender capital for their high-end clients, but also to articulate how our algorithmically-designed platforms mitigate risk in a way that no other premium financing intermediary can.

If you go to my website – *LionsmarkCapital.com* – and click on *About Us*, you can watch interview videos of some of the top financial advisors, CPAs, attorneys, and carriers talking about their experiences doing business with me.

In closing, I will reiterate the importance of not only understanding *The Probability Of Risk*, but more importantly, *The Consequence Of Risk*. If you are a client that is considering using an *IUL* as a wealth building or generational wealth preservation strategy, you owe it to your family to insist that the agent you decide to work with is able to do the due diligence I have described in this book and model a range of scenarios with volatility and pessimistic assumptions.

And if you are a life insurance agent or financial advisor that is considering recommending *IULs* to your clients, I cannot emphasize enough the importance of learning from an expert that truly understands these concepts and can articulately communicate these variables to your clients. Making a big life insurance sale is great, but it is far more important to make sure you are doing the right thing for the client, and if you can mathematically prove that your recommendation is not only appropriate, but superior to all other available alternative options, you are providing an invaluable service to your clients.

For more information about Darren Sugiyama, visit:
DarrenSugiyama.com

For more information about how to use an
IUL for retirement purposes, visit:
Rothish.com

For more information about Lionsmark Capital, visit:
LionsmarkCapital.com

IUL FOR ASPIRING KNOW-IT-ALLS

This is the 12th book Darren Sugiyama has authored, with many of his published works being distributed in Australia, Brasil, Canada, Croatia, Czechoslovakia, Denmark, India, Italy, Japan, New Zealand, Norway, Singapore, Sweden, the United Kingdom, and the United States of America. Darren lives with his wife Emilia and his son Estevan in Orange County, California.

www.ingramcontent.com/pod-product-compliance
Lightning Source LLC
Chambersburg PA
CBHW072204170526
45158CB00004BB/1757